Fear of Freedom
Carlo Levi

Translated by Adolphe Gourevitch

With the essay "Fear of Painting"

Edited with Notes and an Introduction by Stanislao G. Pugliese

T0385559

Columbia University Press / New York

Columbia University Press
Publishers Since 1893
New York

First English edition published as *Of Fear and Freedom*,
copyright © 1950, 1977 Farrar, Straus and Giroux, Inc.

Revised edition copyright © 2008 Columbia University Press

Sergio Amaro's chronology of Levi's life is adapted from
Fleeting Rome: In Search of La Dolce Vita, by Carlo Levi,
translated by Antony Shugaar, copyright 2004, reproduced
by permission of John Wiley & Sons Limited.

Library of Congress Cataloging-in-Publication Data
Levi, Carlo, 1902–1975.
    [Paura della libertà. English]
    Fear of freedom : with the essay, "Fear of painting" / Carlo Levi ;
translated by Adolphe Gourevitch ; edited with notes and an
introduction by Stanislao G. Pugliese.   Rev. ed.
        p. cm.
    Includes bibliographical references.
    ISBN 978-0-231-13996-0 (cloth) —
    ISBN 978-0-231-13997-7   (pbk.)
    1. Religion. 2. Art—Philosophy. 3. Levi, Carlo, 1902–1975   Art.
    I. Pugliese, Stanislao G., 1965– II. Levi, Carlo, 1902–1975.
    Paura della pittura. English. III. Title.
BL50.L413   2008
    200   dc22   2007037041

Fear of Freedom

Contents

Illustrations

Translator's Preface

I t is not usual for a translator to speak in his own name. But this is a rather unusual book, and the job of preparing a version for the American reader has been quite an adventure in itself—which may or may not justify a few words of explanation (about the Italian original) and an apology (about the "translation").

Carlo Levi's *Paura della libertà*—*Fear of Freedom*, or rather: *Of Fear and Freedom*—is a short book, almost a booklet, which does not solve but does clearly state the biggest problem in the world, the most important question, fact or figure man has ever had to consider: namely, himself. The subject of this shrewd historical analysis, or study of social psychology, the hero of this epic poem and sacred drama, is nothing and nobody in particular, everything, everybody in general: our father Adam, you and I, your folks and mine, the collective and the individual monster.

Monster: as every word in this author's language, one must take it at its face value, remembering that a value, not unlike Janus, has always more than one face. Man is still the greatest beast in paradise, the marvel of creation wherever he looks. And whenever he looks upon himself, at his own world, upon the surface of all the waters and deep into every sky, he shrinks away from his own image, and replaces it by another image of his own, by another *idol*; by the ambiguousness of his gracious and fearful gods, the gods of ambiguity.

And here comes Carlo Levi, going into the very depth of the mirror without making faces. He describes what he sees—which is a work of wisdom. And he pictures it as he sees it, which is a work of beauty. For Carlo Levi is a physician and a painter, a writer and fighter for liberty—that is true. But mainly he is a genius: like the child in Andersen's tale, he can tell a king by his nakedness, and draw a masterpiece out of it.

To what literary genre does this book belong? Classifying would be idleness. *Of Fear and Freedom*—in our humble judgment—pertains to science as well as poetry: which in all of Adam's days were not, or should not have been divided.

It would be even less useful to define the author's philosophy, or political opinions, or general credo. The critic's guesses—if any—might be as good or bad as our own comments. The true reader shall read this little book time and again (at least as far as the original is concerned) and may be trusted to find the answers by himself. However, the vast majority of those who will not read it at all, or peruse it only once, might feel too certain about the writer's views and conclusions. And therefore, perhaps, a warning is not quite superfluous.

Although Carlo Levi describes the history, society and psychology of man from the starting point of religion, he is by no means a religious philosopher, nor a mere sociologist of religion, nor a believer in any definite deity. And while he exposes each and every idol, Carlo Levi should not be mistaken for an iconoclast, as he shows the inevitable, the legitimate function of idolatry in every religion—be it a church or a state, or the most private, personal faith and intimate conviction.

This book contains a lucid, fearless, ruthless, sometimes impudent criticism—an unanswerable criticism—of everything man adores: himself and his woman, his individual and collective self, the mass and the race, the class and the state, their freedom and slavery, their peace and their wars. This is a light which illuminates the dark foundations, but does not burn down the great temple of Adam. A remorseless, poetical light, revealing at one stroke the eternal outlines. A vision through every sacred dogma of virtue and love, of social utopism and national pride. A vivisection of clannishness and feudalism, monarchy and revolution, of all the fascisms and all the liberations.

But nowhere does the author give preference to his own ideals or idols of liberty. He does not preach and propagate a doctrine of his own, nor plead for any particular form of salvation, nor state peremptorily any universal truth. Except maybe the one which "manifests *itself* before the open eyes": a truth too naked for the taste of our generation, or of any generation since the great fall.

For "night's darkness dwells in the depth of man: upon the works of man the sun is shining."

Every translation is a betrayal. Especially in the case of a booklet of such magnitude. Therefore, our first reflection, when asked by our friend Carlo Levi to put the thing into English without betraying it, was—after careful reading and pondering—to refuse energetically. But once the poison is in the blood, there is no other cure but to pass it on; and so we undertook the task, with passion and almost with despair, struggling through a few sentences a day, and playing with the golden words of Italy—in the hope of conveying to the American reader some faint image of this gem of beauty, some idea about this wise poem of timeless truth.

It has been worked in the style of the Mediterranean, a style of which Carlo Levi is a peculiar master, and in which the delicate and intricate precision of Latin expression blends with the ancient powers of the Hebrew word. A sensuous and musical sorcery of logic and magic at once.

There was no hope of translating it into real American, into the vernacular of the state—whose great qualities and particular limitations differ entirely from those required; a language, anyhow, into which a writer must be born, for no stranger can possibly *learn* it. So the only way open was to make use of a historical peculiarity which distinguishes literary English: its ability to swallow up an extraordinary amount of Latin forms and words without losing its own identity and without becoming utterly incomprehensible.

We do not claim, therefore, to have *translated* this Latin song of Adam, but only to have rephrased it to the point where any cultured

American (who does not know the Italian language) may listen to it without undue effort, and feels its rhythm and melody, both philosophical and verbal, and gain at least an inkling of what he has lost by not being able to hear the original Italian.

A. G.

Author's Preface

I wrote this book in a time which seems already remote, not so much because of the seven years that have passed, but because of the many events that took place within this short period. To those men who in some peculiar and often miraculous manner have survived, these events, whether unexpected or not, brought an experience of suffering, of blood and of death such as cannot be measured by the common yardstick of time. And today, that which was happening prior to this interlude of slaughter seems gone forever, even if perchance our thoughts have not changed, or we have taken again to our old habits, and found once more the ways of long ago.

It was then that the crisis which was beclouding the life of Europe for several decades, and which had manifest itself in all the rifts, problems, difficulties, cruelties, heroism and tedium of our time, resolved itself into a catastrophe.

War had begun, the German armored divisions were overrunning the plains of Poland. From my house on the shore of the Atlantic I could watch daily the incoming English troopships, which were disembarking the first British army in the harbor of Saint Nazaire.

The French soldiers were leaving, in their shabby uniforms with the fustian trousers, wearing the annoyed faces of pacifists vowed to defeat; the English were arriving, a sixteenth-century army from a revived *Merry England*, drunken and impudent, amateur warriors who were the terror of the Catholic women of Brittany, and cheerfully sure of victory, no matter how remote.

Traditional military values seemed entirely upset: but not only military values. All the data of a civilization were dissolving in mist; an uncertain future was lying in wait, uncertain for the world, and uncertain for each individual. The old ideologies, all of them, were apparently collapsing, exhausted by sterile criticism and by futile defense: a wind of death and of obscure religion was shaking the ancient states of Europe.

On the beach of La Baule the wind was blowing and lifting with a slight rustle the white subtle shells, tenuous skeletons of the dead leaves of the sea. The past was fading away as into another life, beyond the chasm of war. Normal life, the continuity of generations and institutions, was at an end. The new gods of the state were blowing away from the world human values and even the sense of time. To protect themselves men had to accept this barren slaughter, to abandon everything they had lived for, and even the memory of childhood's ties.

It was then that I was informed of the unexpected death of my father: the closed borders had prevented me from seeing him before the end. At this point of life where there was no turning back, I found myself alone on a deserted beach, in a bleak autumn, full of wind and rain.

The past being dead, the present uncertain and frightful, the future dark with mystery, one felt the need to look around and take one's bearings; to stop and consider the reasons for the bloody revolution which was taking shape.

Thus I resolved to write (for myself alone and without any thought of publication, for at that time such a thought would have been quite absurd) a book which according to its first outline should have been rather lengthy: after a general description of the contemporary crisis in its entirety (for I had no doubts about the strict interdependency of its various aspects), there was to be a series of analyses, taking up each problem separately. In other words, the book would have consisted of an introduction, showing the common deep causes of the crisis, and seeking them not so much in this or that particular event, but rather in the very soul of man; and of many chapters dealing with each single subject from politics (with a critical analysis of ideologies, both liberal and socialist) and art (including a history of modern art) to science, philosophy, religion, technical progress, social life, customs, etc.

I began to write under the conditions described, with the poetic pleasure of discovery. I had no books at my disposal, and no documentation pertaining to any of the particular problems. After I had written the first eight chapters I was forced to interrupt my work and return to Paris. In the following months I had no time to write; then there followed the defeat of the French and the flight before Hitler's armies. The Germans entered Paris, the German flag was hoisted upon the Eiffel Tower, on that fourteenth of June which may well remain as a symbolic date marking the end of a world of civilization, of art, of culture, a world that will never come back, even if today it does not seem to have been replaced by anything else of a definite character.

I was not able to continue the book because of these external obstacles; but also, and chiefly, because I noticed that such as it was, my book—for me—was finished. What I had written was approximately the introduction or the preface to the work outlined above, but all the particular developments which I had in mind were implicit therein. I had tried to reach the core of the world I was describing, to immerse myself in that ambiguous hell: because of this writing *from the inside*, the style of the book had assumed a poetic and religious character which arose directly from its subject. Considering this effort to achieve identification and unity (in addition to the practical reasons, obvious to anybody who was writing at that time in European countries subject to tyranny, where the art of allusion had become the most important of all literary expedients), I felt that the book already contained everything I intended to state, and that it ought not be developed in a more explicit way. There was in it a theory of Nazism, although Nazism is not mentioned even once by name; there was a theory of the state and liberty; there was a theory of esthetics, of religion, of sin, etc. The book remained as it was, without addition. I brought it, secretly, to Italy in 1941; and many friends advised me to publish it at once. But, of course, no Italian publisher could at that time take the risk of these too obvious symbols.

Recently, after seven years, and after all that has happened, I had to decide whether it was still worth while to publish it, and if so, whether I ought to postpone the publication, to transpose the book into expository language, into political and historical terms, and to reveal the symbols (already quite transparent) by adding to them all the results of accumulated experience. But, quite apart from the fact that such an improvement and transposition would be very difficult for me, or even impossible, it seemed to me that it was preferable not to change the manuscript at all, so that it would retain the character of a document about a time in which we have lived with such intensity. The book—as I have said—was written for me alone, without any thought of publication: therefore it has the characteristics of a "confession." Certain lands thus discovered are not visited twice; and there is a world of present activities which prevents us from plunging again into that lake of barbarism, from re-entering that forest, those Middle Ages of the soul. Therefore I have refrained from changing even one word in the original draft, and from correcting even those parts which seem to me the weakest and the least ready for immediate publication. It appeared to me that this little book (so different from my *Christ Stopped at Eboli*, which was written five years later) should be allowed to keep its own time element, for in this time element, perhaps resides its value of expression. If I am wrong, I beg the reader to forgive me.

C. L.

Rome, January 1946

Acknowledgments

I am indebted to Jonathan Galassi and Michael Hathaway of Farrar, Straus & Giroux for their gracious permission to reprint the English translation of Levi's *Fear of Freedom*, first published in the United States by FSG in 1950. Tragically, the work seems as relevant today as it was when it first appeared. I would also like to thank Mark Rotella for his support and his introduction to a new edition of Levi's *Christ Stopped at Eboli* published by FSG in 2006. Wendy Lochner, Christine Mortlock, and Michael Haskell at Columbia University Press guided this project through to publication. A Puffin Foundation Grant and the Kirsch Endowment at Hofstra University were used to defray costs associated with reproducing Levi's artwork. I am grateful to Carman Pugliese for reproducing the illustrations. For some notes to the text, I have made use of Adolphe Gourevitch's detective work; for the translation of the Latin texts, I am indebted to my colleague Dr. John A. Walsh of the History Department at Hofstra University. My thanks to David Ward of Wellesley College and Lawrence Baldassaro of the University of Wisconsin at Milwaukee for their impressive scholarship on Carlo Levi and their suggestions for the select bibliography. Antony Shugaar and Dr. Rosa Zagari-Marinzoli of the College of New Jersey and Giovanna Faleschini-Lerner at Franklin and Marshall College corrected many mistakes in my translation of "Fear of Painting"; I have not always adopted their suggestions, so any mistakes that remain are strictly my own. In Italy, I was fortunate to have the assistance of former president of the Fondazione Carlo Levi in Rome, Dr. Pia Vivarelli, and the current president, Dr. Antonella Lavorgna. This project was made possible by a grant from Hofstra University and the support of Dr. Bernard J. Firestone, dean of the College of Liberal Arts and Sciences, and Dr. Herman A. Berliner, vice president and provost of Hofstra University. Finally I must mention my debt to Jennifer Romanello and our children Alessandro Antonio and Giulia Rosina; I trust they will understand.

Stanislao G. Pugliese
March 2007

Sketch for the logo of the Florentine publishing house La Nuova Italia
(1945).

Introduction: Fear of Freedom and the Eternal Tendency Toward Fascism

Stanislao G. Pugliese

Every age has its own fascism.—Primo Levi

When Carlo Levi's *Paura della libertà* was first published in Italy in 1946, critics were puzzled and disappointed: was this the same Carlo Levi whose extraordinary *Cristo si è fermato a Eboli* had appeared the previous year? With its concrete imagery and compassionate ethnography, that earlier book had won over not only the Italian literary establishment and its various political currents, but the larger public as well. *Fear of Freedom* seemed to have been written by an entirely different author. And yet there is a clear genealogy between the two; indeed, *Fear of Freedom* must be recognized as the interpretive key to understanding Levi's entire oeuvre.[1]

Fear of Freedom is a work that is *sui generis*. Levi meant it to serve as an introduction to a larger work, perhaps a Spenglerian or Toynbean grand master narrative. The war disrupted that plan, and Levi never returned to complete the larger project, perhaps recognizing the impossibility of such a narrative after Auschwitz and Hiroshima. It some ways, his elegiac postwar novel *L'orologio* (*The Watch*, 1950) took up this meditation on time, memory, and history in a different, more intimate form.

Written as war clouds were gathering over Europe, *Fear of Freedom* is a lyrical and metaphysical thinking through of man's flight from moral and spiritual autonomy and the resulting loss of self and creativity. As he watched British troops disembark in the fall of 1939 near the coast of La Baule, on the Atlantic coast of western

France not far from Nantes, Levi brooded on what surely appeared to be the decline, if not the fall of Europe as the German armies prepared to eviscerate an entire world. "A large, absurd moon reigns over these solitary beaches," he wrote in a melancholy letter on September 30, 1939, "it is the place most propitious to memories and the remembrance of lost times."[2] Exiled from Italy because of his antifascism, Levi was unable to assist his father on his deathbed and could not attend his father's funeral. This only partially accounts for the book's melancholy. In many ways, Levi here anticipated ideas put forth later by a wide range of Western intellectuals: social psychologist of the Frankfurt School Erich Fromm, Italian semiotician Umberto Eco, cultural critic Susan Sontag, historian Robert O. Paxton, essayist Lewis Lapham, and, most recently, literary critic Terry Eagleton.[3] Levi avoids the rhetoric of analysis or political science and instead approaches the problem through more poetic language, employing a lexicon of metaphor, symbolism, poetry, and mythology. Without access to a library but with references to the entire intellectual and cultural patrimony of Western civilization (from the Bible and Greek mythology to Freud and Jung; from the eighteenth-century counter-Enlightenment Neapolitan philosopher Giambattista Vico to Friedrich Nietzsche), Levi's book is a profound mythopoeic meditation on the paradoxical relationship between human beings, freedom, and the creative process. Levi's work is not only a meditation on a specific moment in history and a universal, timeless condition, but today reads as a powerful indictment of our own contemporary moral and political failures.

Carlo Levi was born (November 29, 1902) into a wealthy, assimilated Jewish family in the northwestern Italian city of Turin.[4] His father, Ercole, was a successful and respected physician and his mother, Annetta Treves, was the sister of Claudio Treves, a leading figure of the Italian Socialist Party. After graduating from the renowned Liceo Alfieri in 1917, he enrolled at the University of Turin and earned a degree in medicine in 1924, though he never officially practiced medicine. Instead, he gravitated toward painting and—in the context of the fascist dictatorship of Benito Mussolini—antifascist politics. The two activities—painting and antifascism—were intimately connected in his mind. Antifascism required a new style of painting, one capable of freeing men and women from fear. Conversely, Levi saw in certain forms of contemporary painting a reflection of an eternal tendency to flee from freedom.

It was during his studies at the University of Turin that Levi befriended Piero Gobetti, the boy wonder of Turinese politics and culture. Gobetti and his young wife, Ada, had attracted the finest young minds of the city to a literary and political circle that would find its voice in two remarkable journals, *Energie Nove* and *La Rivoluzione Liberale*. The former began publication in November 1918 as the Great War came to an end; the latter in February 1922 as fascist blackshirts rampaged through the streets of Italy. Levi embraced Gobetti's thesis that Italy, never having fully experienced the great transformative events of modernity such as the religious, political, scientific, and intellectual revolutions of the seventeenth and eighteenth centuries, had never really reached political "maturity." It was through Gobetti that Levi came to know a Sardinian intellectual transplanted into the soil of Turin: Antonio Gramsci, a founding member of the Italian Communist Party (PCI). With Gramsci's Ordine Nuovo group complementing Gobetti's, Turin gained a well-deserved reputation as one of the most antifascist of Italian cities. Gobetti's brilliant mind and pen caught the attention of Mussolini himself, who sent a telegram to the local fascist authorities that the young antifascist should be "taught a lesson." The subsequent beating in September 1925 left lasting damage that contributed to Gobetti's early death in Paris a few months later. Levi had by then accepted Gobetti's condemnation that fascism was no mere parenthesis in Italian history nor an aberration but "the autobiography of a nation": a nation that rejected the necessary compromise of politics; a nation that worshiped unanimity; a nation that feared heresy.[5]

In the mid-1920s Levi briefly worked in the medical field, conducting experiments on liver disease and the bile ducts and completing postgraduate studies in Paris. The City of Lights, though,

was far more important in introducing Levi to contemporary painters such as the Fauvists, the postimpressionists, and Amedeo
Modigliani and Giorgio De Chirico. Levi set up a studio in Paris
and continued to experiment, not with livers and bile ducts but
with form, composition, and color on canvas. As early as 1924, two
years into the fascist era, Levi was able to exhibit his work at the
fourteenth Venice Biennale. Notwithstanding his well-known antifascism, he continued to exhibit at the Venice Biennales of 1926,
1930, and 1932. Paris was fundamental in his intellectual and cultural development; there he forged friendships not only with painters but also with Stravinsky, Prokofiev, and a wide panoply of European intellectuals. Paris was to leave a lasting mark of creativity
and melancholy on Levi. It was in Paris that Gobetti died, and it
was in Paris that Levi's uncle, Claudio Treves, hounded out of Italy
by the fascists, also went to die in 1933.

In addition to his relationships with Gobetti and Gramsci, another crucial friendship was that with the Rosselli brothers, Carlo
and Nello. Carlo Rosselli, a founder of a new political movement,
Giustizia e Libertà (Justice and Liberty), was one of the most charismatic and influential of European antifascist intellectuals. Many
considered him to be the enfant terrible of European antifascism.
Born into a wealthy Jewish family, and abandoning a promising
career as a professor of political economics, Rosselli devoted his
considerable fortune and ultimately his life to the struggle against
fascism. In 1925, he was instrumental in establishing the first un-
derground antifascist newspaper, Non Mollare! (Don't give in!). For
assisting in the expatriation of the Filippo Turati, the "grand old
man" of Italian socialism, Rosselli had been sentenced, as would
Levi later, to confino, or domestic exile, in the Italian south. There,
he wrote his major theoretical work, Liberal Socialism, arguing that
socialism was the logical development of the principle of liberty.
After a daring escape from the island of Lipari, he made his way
to Paris and became the driving force behind Justice and Liberty.
With Rosselli's brother, the historian Nello Rosselli, and Riccardo
Bauer, Carlo Levi founded a new journal in Turin, La lotta politica,
in 1929. If Carlo Levi represented an intellectual resistance against

fascism, Carlo Rosselli was the epitome of the antifascist activist. He was among the first to arrive in Barcelona after the outbreak of the Spanish Civil War, in which he commanded an armed column of volunteers in defense of the Republic. When the secret police learned of Rosselli's plan to expand the Spanish Civil War into a preemptive strike against fascist Italy and Nazi Germany and discovered his plot to assassinate Mussolini, they declared him "the regime's most dangerous enemy" and had him murdered, along with his brother Nello, on a country road in Normandy. The assassination became the basis for Alberto Moravia's novel *The Conformist* as well as the film of the same name by Bernardo Bertolucci.[6] Levi, intellectually and emotionally close to both brothers, worked through his grief by painting a revealing *Self-Portrait with Bloody Shirt*.

Levi was attracted to the radical new ideology of Justice and Liberty. The movement stressed that, unlike the other antifascist parties such as the Italian Socialist Party (PSI) and the Italian Communist Party (PCI), which had their roots in a prefascist Italy, Justice and Liberty was the only movement that arose directly in response to Mussolini's regime. It was not tied to schemata and rigid ideologies and therefore attracted a heterogeneous group of intellectuals. Levi was, together with Leone Ginzburg, Vittorio Foa, Augusto Monti, Aldo Garosci, Gobetti's extraordinary widow, Ada, and others, one of the leaders of Justice and Liberty in Turin. Later the Turin branch would welcome writer Cesare Pavese and chemist Primo Levi. Ginzburg and Carlo Levi were given the task of reaching out to the youth in Italy, who, after more than a decade of fascism, had known no other political system. It was because of Levi's experience in *confino* in Basilicata that these northern Italian intellectuals were forced to confront the seemingly intractable problem of *meridionalismo*, or "the Southern Question," which had first been broached by Guido Dorso, Gaetano Salvemini, and Giustino Fortunato.[7] When Justice and Liberty was accused of vague ideas and an inarticulate antifascism, Levi worked with Carlo Rosselli, Emilio Lussu, Alberto Tarchiani, and others in drafting the "Revolutionary Program of Justice and Liberty."[8]

"Fascism" they wrote, "cannot be defeated except by a revolutionary movement that decisively imposes and resolves, by the use of freedom, the fundamental political and social problems of Italian life." Justice and Liberty was "the concrete expression" of the forces that struggle on the revolutionary terrain against fascism. Justice and Liberty argued for an end to the monarchy and for the widest possible forms of democracy and autonomy, based essentially on the working classes. Italy's myriad social problems could be traced to the questions of land reform, industrial relations, and factory organization, reflecting the influence of Gobetti and Gramsci. Unlike the antifascists grouped around liberal philosopher Benedetto Croce, Justice and Liberty argued that the prefascist past was no model for an antifascist and postfascist Italy. In fact, the more radical theorists of Justice and Liberty, such as Rosselli and Levi, argued that prefascist Italy was directly responsible for the politically monstrous birth of fascism. There could be, they argued, no nostalgic "return to the past."

The first order of business was to end the monarchy, establish a Republic, and reestablish all the political, social, and civil liberties that had been abolished by the fascist regime. There was to be a purge of fascists, and those who had profited from the widespread corruption of the regime were to be prosecuted. Political prisoners were to be immediately released from detention, whether in prison or in *confino*. Justice and Liberty adopted the slogan, "Land to those who work it." Industry was not to be completely nationalized but organized as a mixed economy. "Sharecroppers, small tenants, leasers and in general all those who cultivate the land with their personal labor or with their family, will acquire the land they cultivate, with a moderate indemnity paid to the old proprietors." (The indemnity clause was later dropped.) "The problem of the industrial crisis, which is not solely economic, but of men and classes cannot be resolved except by a general re-organization of industry and the transformation of internal relations within the factory." Essential public services would be socialized.

"Workers' control" (again demonstrating the influence of Gobetti and Gramsci) would be introduced in all the large and medium firms, public as well as private. This would ensure to the working classes "an effective participation in management" and "affirm workers' freedom in the factory, to develop the industrial capacity of the working class, and to oppose, in the interest of production, the tendencies toward bureaucratization and centralization." The property of the fascist party and organizations was to be confiscated and transferred to worker and peasant organizations. There would be unemployment insurance and a minimum wage. Justice and Liberty advocated a foreign policy of peace and disarmament with greatly reduced military and colonial spending and "freedom for the inhabitants of the colonies." There was to be "a united organization of Europe" and cultural and administrative autonomy for ethnic minorities in places like Alto Adige. The program insisted on independence and lifetime tenure for judges along with a radical reform of the prison system. Education was to be free, while "teaching and culture will receive the maximum impulse and will be considered as essential to the life and progress of the Republic." Contrary to the recently concluded Lateran Accords between the Catholic Church and the fascist regime, there was to be "complete separation" of Church and the state, confiscation of Church property, and "unconditional freedom of conscience and worship."

In some ways, Justice and Liberty and its political heir during the period of the armed Resistance (1943–1945), the Action Party, were to be more radical than the PCI. For example, the leader of the PCI, Palmiro Togliatti, refused to support this last point of abrogating the Lateran Accords or the purge of fascists after the war.

Justice and Liberty soon became known as the "party of intellectuals"; in fact, its great flaw was its difficulty in attracting factory workers, artisans, the bourgeoisie, and peasants. More ominously, in the reports of the fascist secret police Justice and Liberty was soon labeled "the party of Jewish intellectuals." When Sion Segre Amar, a young idealistic man from Turin approached Carlo Levi about joining the movement, Levi could only moan, "Alas, another Jew." Levi made it clear to the young man that he didn't want Justice and Liberty to be known as a "Jewish" movement. Segre wittily asked if he should first convert to Catholicism to join, or should he

Sketch for the emblem of the Action Party
with the flaming sword of Giustizia e Libertà (1944).

become a fascist just because he was a Jew? [9] Amar was clear on
why Italian Jews were attracted to Justice and Liberty: "They felt
fascism as an obstacle to their own ideologies and in Justice and
Liberty they found a force (though very modest) for the struggle
against that obstacle, but without mental constrictions or excessively rigid programs."[10]

While it is often argued that Italian fascism adopted anti-Semi-
tism only with the Racial Laws of 1938, the regime equated Judaism with antifascism as early as 1934.[11] The semiofficial newspaper
of the regime, Telesio Interlandi's *Il Tevere* of Rome, commented
that "the best of antifascism, past and present, is of the Jewish
race: from Treves to Modigliani, from Rosselli to Morgari, the or-
ganizers of antifascist subversion were and are members of 'the
chosen people.'"[12] A spy who infiltrated the Turin branch of Justice

and Liberty and noted the significant contributions of Carlo Levi, Leone Ginzburg, and others, concluded one report with the observation, "One senses easily existing among them a common link derived from race (they are all Jews)."[13]

The Turin branch of Justice and Liberty was deeply immersed in the cultural battle raging within Italy during the 1930s. Levi's practice of painting portraits in his Turin studio offered ample time and sufficient cover to discuss antifascism with others. Under the patronage of Giulio Einaudi and the Einaudi publishing house, Carlo Levi, Leone Ginzburg, Cesare Pavese, and Luigi Salvatorelli came together to form a new journal, *La Cultura*. Levi there signed his work with the nom de plume "Tre Stelle" (Three Stars).

On March 13, 1934, Levi was arrested for his participation in Justice and Liberty. An appeal was launched from the pages of the antifascist newspaper *La Libertà* for his release, signed by Léger, Chagall, Derain, Signac, and others. On May 9, the regime released Levi, placing him on probation for two years. His formal request for the drawings he completed in prison, though, was denied.

In the spring of 1935, Levi and most of the Turinese group were betrayed by a police spy and arrested by the fascists.[14] Levi was first interrogated then sent to Rome's notorious Regina Coeli prison. Two months after his arrest he was sentenced to three years of *confino* in the small town of Grassano in the remote southern region of Basilicata. In September, based on the recommendation of the prefect of Matera, Levi was moved to the town of Aliano. During his confinement, he was permitted to receive visitors, the most important being his sister Luisa and his lover, Paola Levi, whose portrait he painted several times (she gave birth to their daughter in 1937).

It was out of the experience of a year in *confino* in Basilicata that, eight years later, in hiding from the Nazis in Florence, Levi was to write his most famous work, a masterpiece of ethnography and human solidarity, *Christ Stopped at Eboli*. For a northern Italian—and a Jew—the experience of the lives of the southern Italian peasants came as a revelation. Levi soon came to recognize that beneath a thin veneer of Christianity lay millennia of pagan culture.

Christ Stopped at Eboli was Levi's way of keeping a promise he had made to "return" to the peasants in Aliano. "Closed in one room, in a world apart, I am glad to travel in my memory to that other part of the world, hedged in by custom and sorrow, cut off from History and the State, eternally patient, to that land without comfort or solace, where the peasant lives out his motionless civilization on the barren ground in remote poverty, and in the presence of death."[15]

Levi derived the title of his book from a timeless aphorism of the peasants: Eboli is a town near the Tyrrhenian coast; the peasants meant that Christ and civilization never made it as far as their poor mountain town. Indeed, the word *cristiani* in the language of the Mezzogiorno meant not so much "Christians" as "civilized" or "decent" people.

> Christ never came this far, nor did time, nor the individual soul, nor hope, nor the relation of cause to effect, nor reason nor history. Christ never came, just as the Romans never came, content to garrison the highways without penetrating the mountains and forests, nor the Greeks, who flourished beside the Gulf of Taranto. None of the pioneers of Western civilization brought here his sense of the passage of time, his deification of the State or that ceaseless activity which feeds upon itself. No one has come to this land except as an enemy, a conqueror, or a visitor devoid of understanding. The seasons pass today over the toil of the peasants, just as they did three thousand years before the birth of Christ; no message, human or divine, has reached this stubborn poverty. We speak a different language, and here our tongue is incomprehensible. The greatest travelers have not gone beyond the limits of their own world; they have trodden the paths of their own souls, of good and evil, of morality and redemption. Christ descended into the underground hell of Hebrew moral principle in order to break down its doors in time and seal them up into eternity. But into this shadowy land, that knows neither sin nor redemption from sin, where evil is not moral but is only the pain residing forever in earthly things, Christ did not come. Christ stopped at Eboli.[16]

Midway through his year of *confino*, Levi was permitted a brief return to Turin to attend the funeral of an uncle. He managed to visit some antifascist friends. Out of that encounter came the realization that there was an unbridgeable abyss, not only between the peasants and the "State" but between a southern Italian reality and its perception by northern Italian intellectuals:

> At bottom, as I now perceived, they were all unconscious worshipers of the State. Whether the State they worshiped was the Fascist State or the incarnation of quite another dream, they thought of it as something that transcended both its citizens and their lives. Whether it was tyrannical or paternalistic, dictatorial or democratic, it remained to them monolithic, centralized, and remote. . . . All of them agreed that the State should do something about [the south], something concretely useful, and beneficent, and miraculous, and they were shocked when I told them that the State, as they conceived it, was the greatest obstacle to the accomplishment of anything. The State, I said, cannot solve the problem of the South, because the problem which we call by this name is none other than the problem of the State itself.
>
> There will always be an abyss between the State and the peasants, whether the State be Fascist, Liberal, Socialist or take on some new form in which the middle-class bureaucracy still survives. We can bridge the abyss only when we succeed in creating a government in which the peasants feel they have some share.[17]

On May 20, 1936, in celebration of the fascist acquisition of an "African Empire" after the defeat of Ethiopia (with the use of poison gas), Levi and other political prisoners were granted an amnesty and released. Levi, though, did not immediately leave Aliano. The year he had spent in Aliano had marked him for life.

Returning to Turin in that spring of 1936, Levi also surreptitiously returned to clandestine political work. With the passage of the fascist regime's anti-Semitic legislation in 1938 and the increasingly close alliance with Nazi Germany, Levi was forced to flee Italy in 1939 and found refuge in France.

Levi, Carlo Rosselli and other members of Justice and Liberty, developed a conception of fascism that would be echoed several decades later in the work of the German-born psychoanalyst and social philosopher Erich Fromm.[18] "Freedom is a burden," Rosselli noted in an unpublished essay. "This duty to keep oneself free, to follow reason and the critical spirit is overwhelming."[19] Italians were lacking neither the political intelligence nor the capacity to create new systems of thought; what was absent, according to Rosselli, was "character, the will to fight, the obstinacy of sacrifice, the coherence between thought and action."[20] Levi agreed, seeing the deep roots of fascism in the "inherited incapacity to be free" and in the "fear of passion and responsibility." The "morally weak" Italians felt a need for "an exterior order" that would replace an "inexistent morality."[21] Emilio Lussu, for his part, agreed with Gobetti, Rosselli, and Levi that the Italians had inherited a moral conscience brutalized by centuries of feudalism and Catholicism. "It is not intelligence that Italians lack; they have enough to export. It is character that is missing."[22] Levi and his colleagues were anticipating Italian liberal philosopher Benedetto Croce's later formulation of fascism as "moral sickness" with roots in rabid nationalism, fanatical imperialism, romantic decadence, and the First World War. Croce was also a senator in the Italian parliament and had initially given his support to fascism, even after the regime was charged with the assassination of the socialist deputy Giacomo Matteotti in 1924. By defining fascism first as a "parenthesis" in the unfolding history of liberty in Italy and then later as a "moral sickness," Croce was crafting a strategy that could deny that there was anything specifically "Italian" about fascism. Levi, Rosselli, and Ferruccio Parri instead condemned the entire experience of liberal Italy, from unification to the Great War, as responsible for the rise of fascism.[23] Levi agreed with Ferruccio Parri's condemnation that "between the Italian State after 1860 and fascism there is a connection; if not of affiliation, of progressive degeneration."[24]

For Levi, there were other forces as well that contributed to the rise of fascism: hundreds of thousands of people who supported the mechanism of the "bureaucratic-dictatorial" state; the cult of violence, a taste for adventure, and authoritarian tendencies generated by the war; a religion of nationalism; weakness of character in the part of the Italians; centuries of servility; the influence of the Church; and political apathy. In short, fascism was both class reaction and moral crisis, and those that fought only the former were fighting only half the battle.[25]

By the manipulation of nationalism, the press, and even sports, the regime could "corrupt and distract" the masses. Sports became the modern circus of the Roman *panem et circenses*. Mussolini had shrewdly realized that control was not a question of smothering every passion, but of directing and channeling those passions in ways favorable to the regime.[26] As Levi discerned in a brilliant essay, "Sport," Italians under fascism had been reduced to individual and private passions such as self-interest and sex (and even these, lamented Levi, "how limited and tired!"). Cinema was a "passive occupation" permitting "easy evasion." The only collective passion left was sport. Sport, which previously had signified initiative, contest, autonomy, and struggle, was antithetical to fascism, but the regime was careful in appropriating whatever it could. Cycling and soccer generated such fanaticism as to be "symptoms of an illness." As Henri De Man had already noted, sports fanaticism was "the principal phenomenon deriving from the repression of instinct generated by the monotonous and brutalizing character of industrial work." For Levi, this enthusiasm could represent something positive (individual fortitude and character in the case of cycling) or collective enterprise (in the case of soccer). But the regime could not permit the expression of such enthusiasm to go uncontrolled. Sport under fascism had become an industry and "cooperated in a most efficacious manner in keeping the country in the beatific state of infancy."[27]

Levi's analysis of future forms of political organization can be seen in the contemporary version of a "media regime":

We cannot foresee the political forms of the future, but in a middle-class country like Italy, where middle-class ideology has infected the masses of workers in the city, it is probable, alas, that the new institutions arising after Fascism, through either gradual evolution or violence, no matter how extreme and revolutionary they may be in appearance, will maintain the same ideology under different forms and create a new State equally far removed from real life, equally idolatrous and abstract, a perpetuation under new slogans and new flags of the worst features of the eternal tendency toward Fascism.[28]

Levi's warning about the "eternal tendency toward fascism" seems ever more prescient. As I write this introduction, Italian newspapers carry a front-page story that former prime minister Silvio Berlusconi has "anointed" neofascist politician Gianfranco Fini his political "heir." In a 1994 interview with the Turin newspaper *La Stampa*, Fini hailed Mussolini as "the greatest statesman of the century." In January 2007, in a perfectly brilliant synthesis of fascism and Christianity, in which Berlusconi morphs into a combined Duce and Christ, he "anoints" Fini his "heir apparent" in what amounts to a symbolic "investiture." And if the reference to his own Christlike essence were not clear enough, Berlusconi remarked that he would happily pass to others such as Fini "the bitter chalice" of political power.[29]

It was not the first time that Berlusconi had (ab)used the fascist past. In an interview with the British journal *The Spectator*, Berlusconi claimed that "Mussolini never killed anyone" and that in the practice of *confino*, the Italian dictator merely sent his political enemies "on holiday" to such idyllic locales as the islands of Lipari and Ponza or quaint hill towns in the Italian south.[30]

During his second stint as prime minister, Berlusconi argued that the nation's history textbooks should be rewritten because they glorify the antifascists. He more than once darkly warned Italy that only he "could save the country from communism."[31] Mussolini, too, had thundered before adoring crowds that only he "could save Italy from the perils of communism." Throughout his political career, Berlusconi constantly and cynically resurrected the specter of communism for reasons of personal expedience, and, in doing so, he raised another ghost, that of fascism. There can be only two possibilities regard-

ing Berlusconi's public remarks that he alone "could save Italy from
the perils of communism": either he is deaf to the irony of his own
rhetoric, or his hearing is pitch-perfect and his comments are instead
a not-so-subtle reference to his own version of "benign" fascism.[32] In
many ways, Levi foresaw the "Berlusconi phenomenon."[33]

For Levi the only solution to the "eternal tendency toward fascism" lay in inventing a new form of government, "neither Fascist,
nor Communist, nor even Liberal, for all three of these are forms
of the religion of the State." Instead, it was imperative that Italy
reconceptualize the concept of the State with the concept of the individual. "For the juridical and abstract concept of the individual we
must substitute a new concept, more expressive of reality, one that
will do away with the now unbridgeable gulf between the individual
and the State." Levi thought he discerned the answer in peasant
civilization. The humanistic yet tragic conception of the individual
that was at the heart of peasant culture was the only path that could
"lead us out of the vicious circle of Fascism and anti-Fascism."[34]

Levi's analysis of fascism is part of a distinguished lineage of political critique. Erich Fromm's *Escape from Freedom*, first published
in 1941, bears an uncanny resemblance to Levi's *Fear of Freedom*.[35]
Fromm (1900–1980) was born in Frankfurt to a family of orthodox
Jews. His father, a wine merchant, was a descendent of rabbis and
Talmudic scholars. In his mid-twenties Erich Fromm abandoned
Orthodox Judaism for humanism and socialism, but traces of his
early religious inspiration can be found in all his later writings. He
earned a doctorate in sociology from the University of Heidelberg in
1922 and then gravitated toward psychoanalysis, opening a private
practice in 1927. In 1930 he joined Frankfurt's Institute for Social
Research and was instrumental in developing the Frankfurt School's
idea of critical theory. He left Germany in 1934, settled in New York
City, and joined the faculty of Columbia University and the University in Exile (forerunner of the present-day New School University), an oasis created for intellectuals fleeing Hitler's Germany and

Nazi-occupied Europe. Struck by the mass hysteria of the First World War and the rise of fascism in Italy and Germany, Fromm's great task was to introduce the indeterminacy of freedom into the relatively deterministic systems of Marx and Freud. The result was a radical, socialist humanism:

> Modern man, freed from the bonds of pre-individualistic society, which simultaneously gave him security and limited him, has not gained freedom in the positive sense of the realization of his individual self; that is, the expression of his intellectual, emotional and sensuous potentialities. Freedom, though it has brought him independence and rationality, has made him isolated and, thereby, anxious and powerless. This isolation is unbearable and the alternatives he is confronted with are either to escape from the burden of this freedom into new dependencies and submission, or to advance to the full realization of positive freedom which is based on the uniqueness and individuality of man.[36]

For Fromm, there was no escaping the fundamental charge of modernity: that as human beings gain freedom by emerging from their dependence on other human beings and nature and by becoming "individuals," they are presented a choice: "unite oneself with the world in the spontaneity of love and productive work" or else seek refuge in a kind of security through such ties with the world as to destroy their freedom and the integrity of their individual selves.[37]

Fromm goes on to draw a direct line of descent between two forms of escaping from freedom: the submission to a leader was the form in fascism, while in our own age it takes the form of compulsive conformity and consumption.[38] For there is "no greater mistake and no graver danger than not to see that in our own society we are faced with the same phenomenon that is fertile soil for the rise of fascism anywhere; the insignificance and powerlessness of the individual."[39] If, as Fromm writes, "democracy is a system that creates the economic, political, and cultural conditions for the full development of the individual," while fascism is a system that, "regardless under which name, makes the individual subordinate to extraneous purposes and weakens the development of genuine individuality,"[40] how many Americans would conclude that we live in a democracy?

Forty-five years after Levi's *Fear of Freedom* first appeared, its message was heard once again, in different form. Speaking at the Casa Italiana of Columbia University in New York City on April 25, 1995, the fiftieth anniversary of the liberation of Italy from the Nazi occupation, Umberto Eco sketched a typology of what he called "Ur-Fascism" or "Eternal Fascism."[41] The first feature of this "eternal fascism," according to Eco was what he termed the "cult of tradition." In this cult, "there can be no advancement of learning. Truth already has been spelled out once and for all, and we can only keep interpreting its obscure message."

Traditionalism, in turn, implies the "rejection of modernism." While traditional thinkers reject technology as "a negation of traditional spiritual values," the fascists and Nazis appeared to "worship" technology. This, though, could not supersede an ideology based upon blood and earth (*Blut und Boden*).[42] "The rejection of the modern world," argues Eco, "was disguised as a rebuttal of the capitalistic way of life. The Enlightenment, the Age of Reason, is seen as the beginning of modern depravity. In this sense Ur-Fascism can be defined as *irrationalism*."

This irrationalism depends on what Eco and others have called the "cult of action for action's sake." Action, being beautiful "in itself," must be taken "before, or without, reflection." Thinking, for the fascist, "is a form of emasculation." Culture is therefore suspect "insofar as it is identified with critical attitudes." Intellectuals, with their fondness for ambiguity and complexity, are not to be trusted. Eco recalls Hermann Goering's apocryphal quip, "When I hear the word 'culture' I reach for my gun." The common contempt for the life of the mind is revealed in such common expressions as "degenerate intellectuals," "eggheads," "effete snobs," and "universities are nests of reds." This produced the oxymoron of "Fascist intellectuals" whose main task was to denigrate "modern culture and the liberal intelligentsia for having betrayed traditional values."

For Eco, "the critical spirit makes distinctions, and to distinguish is a sign of modernism." This, of course, can not be countenanced by fascism. The hallmark of science and modernism is "disagreement as a way to improve knowledge," but for the fascist, *disagreement is treason.*

Not only is disagreement treason, but it is also a sign of "diversity," a quality that cannot be accepted by fascism. "Ur-Fascism," Eco notes, "seeks consensus by exploiting and exacerbating the natural *fear of difference.*" Hence the primordial cry of fascism is "an appeal against the intruders." Eternal Fascism is "racist by definition."

Unable to obtain the obscure object of its desire, Ur-Fascism springs from eternal individual and social frustration. This generates the appeal to a frustrated middle class suffering from either economic crisis or the sting of political humiliation. This class is terrified by the demands of those "below" it. This "in-betweeness" denies the middle class a clear social identity. To these people and others who feel "deprived" of such a comfort, fascism offers a manufactured social privilege: an identity constructed on the radical otherness of those outside the artificial boundaries created by the nation-state. Hence the "invention of tradition" and the origins of nationalism. The result is that "the only ones who can provide an identity to the nation are its enemies." Undergirding fascist social psychology is the *obsession with a plot.* The fascists revel in feeling besieged. And the "easiest way to solve the plot is the appeal to xenophobia."

Fascism tells its followers that they are being "humiliated by the ostentatious wealth and force of their enemies." Eco recalls as a boy in fascist Italy being told that the English were the "five-meal people," in contrast to the "poor but sober Italians." The Jews, on the other hand, "are rich and help each other through a secret web of mutual assistance." But the wealth and power of their enemies can be overcome by the purity of spirit. Thus, "by a continuous shifting of rhetorical focus, the enemies are at the same time too strong and too weak." The resulting paradox is why "fascist governments are condemned to lose wars because they are constitutionally incapable of objectively evaluating the force of the enemy."

Those wars are the inevitable consequence of the idea that "there is no struggle for life but, rather, life is lived for struggle." Life is *permanent warfare.* Pacifism, therefore *is trafficking with the enemy.* The result is an "Armageddon complex." Since enemies must be defeated, there must be "a final battle." Such "final solutions" imply a future "era of peace, a Golden Age, which contradicts the principle of permanent war."

An aristocratic and military elitism embedded in Ur-Fascism implies *contempt for the weak.* But "there cannot be patricians without plebeians." The Duce, the Führer, the Leader, "knowing that his power was not delegated to him democratically but was conquered by force, also knows that his force is based upon the weakness of the masses; they are so weak as to need and deserve a ruler." In such a vision of the world, *everybody is educated to become a hero.* This cult of heroism is "strictly linked with the cult of death. . . . The Ur-Fascist hero craves heroic death, advertised as the best reward for a heroic life. The Ur-Fascist hero is impatient to die. In his impatience, he more frequently sends other people to death."

Permanent war and the call to heroism being difficult "games to play," the Ur-Fascist transfers *his will to power to sexual matters.* From this is machismo born: "disdain for women and intolerance and condemnation of nonstandard sexual habits, from chastity to homosexuality." But even at the game of sex, the Ur-Fascist cheats and "tends to play with weapons," an "ersatz phallic exercise."

The selective populism of fascism insists that individuals, as individuals, possess no inherent rights. Individuals do not exist; only the People, "conceived as a quality, a monolithic entity expressing the Common Will," exists. Since individuals do not exist, the Leader takes upon himself the burden and responsibility—and the fiction—of being their interpreter. The subjects (there can be no citizens) of fascism "are only called on to play the role of the People," a "theatrical fiction." Eco foresaw a "TV or Internet populism, in which the emotional response of a selected group of citizens can be presented and accepted as the Voice of the People."

Ur-Fascism must be against "rotten" parliamentary governments. "Wherever a politician casts doubt on the legitimacy of a

Untitled (Mussolini with skeletal owl, 1944–45)

parliament because it no longer represents the Voice of the People, we can smell Ur-Fascism."

Finally, recalling Orwell, Eco writes that Eternal Fascism *speaks Newspeak*. Ur-Fascism must insist on an "impoverished vocabulary, and an elementary syntax, in order to limit the instruments for complex and critical reasoning." But, Eco warned, "we must be ready to identify other kinds of Newspeak, even if they take the apparently innocent form of a popular talk show."

"Ur-Fascism," cautioned Eco, "is still around us, sometimes in plainclothes." Unfortunately, we often fail to recognize it. Fascism can reappear "under the most innocent of disguises." It is our moral and political task "to uncover it and to point our finger at any of its new instances—every day, in every part of the world." To his American audience, Eco recalled the admonition of President Franklin D. Roosevelt on November 4, 1938: "If American democracy ceases to move forward as a living force, seeking day and night by peaceful means to better the lot of our citizens, fascism will grow in strength in our land." Freedom and liberation, Eco concluded, were not gifts bestowed from above; they must instead be reconceptualized as "an unending task."

Eco's typology of an eternal fascism is echoed in historian Robert Paxton's most recent work, *The Anatomy of Fascism*. Here, Paxton fully develops arguments first broached in a seminal essay, "The Five Stages of Fascism,"[43] and sums up a lifelong reflection on fascism's myriad forms. Fascism, argues Paxton, was "the most self-consciously visual of all political forms," yet many of those indelible images (think of Mussolini or Hitler haranguing a crowd from a balcony or what I would term the perfect "choreography of totalitarianism" found in Leni Riefenstahl's *Triumph of the Will*) can easily "induce facile errors."[44] Most provocative is Paxton's delineation of fascism's "mobilizing passions":[45]

1. A sense of overwhelming crisis beyond the reach of any traditional solutions
2. The primacy of the group, toward which one has duties superior to every right, whether individual or universal, and the subordination of the individual to it
3. The belief that one's group is a victim, a sentiment that justifies any action, without legal or moral limit, against its enemies, both internal and external
4. Dread of the group's decline under the corrosive effects of individualistic liberalism, class conflict, and alien influences
5. The need for closer integration of a purer community, by consent if possible, or by exclusionary violence if necessary

6. The need for authority by natural leaders (always male), culminating in a national chief who alone is capable of incarnating the group's destiny
7. The superiority of the leader's instincts over abstract and universal reason
8. The beauty of violence and the efficacy of will, when they are devoted to the group's success
9. The right of the chosen people to dominate others without restraint from any kind of human or divine law, right being decided by the sole criterion of the group's prowess within a Darwinian struggle

Paxton did not make the explicit connection, but on first reading these lines, my immediate thought went not to the Italy and Germany of the 1930s but to contemporary America. From the permanent "war on terror" to "you're either with us or against us" to the proposed wall on U.S.-Mexico border to 9/11 to the mantra of the radio and talk-show religion that "liberalism = treason" to George "I don't read newspapers" Bush to an official military policy of "shock and awe" to our true religion of American exceptionalism and triumphalism (from "the City on the Hill" to "the New American Century" to a belief that "we create our own reality"), Paxton's "mobilizing passions" seem an accurate diagnosis of a politics that dare not speak its name in contemporary America.

This is not the first time that someone had discerned the dark star of fascism in America. Just as Carlo Levi was witnessing the beginning of World War II on the coast of France in 1939, John Dewey perceived a threat closer to home. "The serious threat to our democracy," the American philosopher wrote, "is not the existence of foreign totalitarian states. It is the existence within our own personal attitudes and within our own institutions of conditions, which have given a victory to external authority, discipline, uniformity and dependence upon The Leader in foreign countries. The battlefield is also accordingly here—within ourselves and our institutions."[46] Dewey pointed to the ambiguous figure of Huey "The Kingfisher" Long in Louisiana who warned (or perhaps boasted) that "Fascism will come to the USA under the name of protecting democracy from its enemies" and that "if fascism ever comes to America, it will come wrapped in an American flag."[47] Sinclair Lewis voiced the same concern in *It Can't Happen Here* (1935).

Dewey was not alone is sensing the danger of fascism on our own shores. In 1940, Henry A. Wallace was Franklin Roosevelt's vice president. Dropped from the electoral ticket in 1944 for being too radical, Wallace shrewdly noted that the American fascist "would prefer not to use violence." The American fascist would prefer to "poison the channels of public information." For the American fascist, the problem is never how to represent the truth, but how to deceive the public. These American fascists are recognized by their "deliberate perversion of truth and fact." They claim to be patriots but "destroy every liberty guaranteed by the Constitution. They demand free enterprise but are the spokesmen for monopoly and vested interest. Their final objective to which all their deceit is directed is to capture political power so that, using the power of the state and the power of the market simultaneously, they may keep the common man in eternal subjection."[48]

This calls to my mind those ominous figures in the back of Plato's cave, throwing shadowy images up before those imprisoned in the cave, who are duped into believing that those images are indeed the truth.

The most recent analysis similar to Levi's is Terry Eagleton's *Holy Terror*. Eagleton opens with a preface that defends this analysis of a "poetics of fascism," or what the author calls a metaphysical or theological turn in the study of fascist terror. "The politics implicit in this rather exotic talk of Satan and Dionysus, scapegoats and demons, are more, not less radical than much that is to be found in the more orthodox discourse of leftism today. . . . The left is at home with imperial power and guerilla warfare, but embarrassed on the whole by the thought of death, evil, sacrifice, or the sublime."[49]

Eagleton echoes Levi when he writes that the concept of terror is intimately linked with that of the *sacred*. "The word *sacer* can

mean either blessed or cursed, holy or reviled; and there are kinds
of terror in ancient civilization which are both creative and destruc-
tive, life-giving and death-dealing. The sacred is dangerous, to be
kept in a cage rather than a glass case."[50]

> The sacred is a Janus-faced power, at once life-giving and death-deal-
> ing, which can be traced all the way from the orgies of Dionysus to the
> shattering elements of the sublime. For late modern civilization, some
> of its primary incarnations are known as the unconscious, the death
> drive, or the Real. This monstrous ambivalence, which for the Judaeo-
> Christian lineage finds its epitome in the holy terror of God, is also to
> be found at the root of the modern conception of freedom. The abso-
> lute notion of freedom, pressed to an extreme limit, involves a form of
> terror which turns against the finitude of the flesh in the very act of
> seeking to serve it. Like the tragic protagonist, it glides through some
> invisible frontier at which its "everything" collapses into nothing.[51]

In a chapter tellingly titled "Fear and Freedom," Eagleton offers
a metaphysical deconstruction of the Western concept of freedom
that sounds as though it were written by Levi himself. Freedom,
he writes, is "the most sublime phenomenon," which, like the god
Dionysius, "is both angel and demon, beauty and terror. If there is
something sacred about liberty it is not only because it is precious,
but because it can destroy as well as create."[52] This is the basis of
understanding our "self-consuming" and infinite war on terror as
"the 'bad' sublime of our own era."[53] The terror of freedom, as Levi
and Eagleton both perceived, lies in its ambiguity.

> Freedom signifies a range of precious human rights, as well as a
> rationale for launching murderous strikes on foreign cities. It is the
> unquenchable spirit of human dignity and the right to shoot unarmed
> domestic intruders through the back. Small farmers are bankrupted
> in its name and hospitals piled high with charred bodies. As an idea
> suspended between the spirit and the flesh, it is one of the few dis-
> courses which can be spoken with equal enthusiasm by archbishops
> and casino owners, oilmen and Oxford philosophers.[54]

Freedom is "this elusive, quicksilver thing" that has the uncanny ability to slip through the "net of representations and can be felt only as a cryptic silence or shadowy presence." Today, we exist in a bewildering epistemological paradox: "As science comes to net more and more truth, philosophy insists that the knower himself, whose essence is freedom, is as inaccessible as the remotest star."[55]

That paradox is reflected in another manner: Freedom is akin to desire, writes Eagleton, echoing Levi. Its realization is a threat to itself. "Only by teetering perpetually on the brink of attainment can [absolute freedom] avoid the disenchantment of fulfillment. It is the exquisite perversity by which we gratify our desire by not enjoying the object of it."[56]

In a seminal essay-review of Leni Riefenstahl's *The Last of the Nuba*, Susan Sontag also echoes Levi's analysis of fascism:

> Fascist aesthetics . . . flow from (and justify) a preoccupation with situations of control, submissive behavior, extravagant effort, and the endurance of pain; they endorse two seemingly opposite states, egomania and servitude. The relations of domination and enslavement take the form of a characteristic pageantry: the massing of groups of people; the turning of people into things; the multiplication or replication of things; and the grouping of people/things around an all-powerful, hypnotic leader-figure or force. The fascist dramaturgy centers on the orgiastic transactions between mighty forces and their puppets, uniformly garbed and shown in ever swelling numbers. Its choreography alternates between ceaseless motion and a congealed, static, "virile" posing. Fascist art glorifies surrender, it exalts mindlessness, it glamorizes death.[57]

And like Levi, Sontag warns that fascism is ever-present. "Fascism," she wrote in 1975,

> stands for an ideal or rather ideals that are persistent today under the other banners: the ideal of life as art, the cult of beauty, the

fetishism of courage, the dissolution of alienation in ecstatic feelings of community; the repudiation of the intellect; the family of man (under the parenthood of leaders). These ideals are vivid and moving to many people, and it is dishonest as well as tautological to say that one is affected by *Triumph of the Will* and *Olympia* only because they were made by a filmmaker of genius. Riefenstahl's films are still effective because, among other reasons, their longings are still felt, because their content is a romantic ideal to which many continue to be attached and which is expressed in such diverse modes of cultural dissidence and propaganda for new forms of community as the youth/rock culture, primal therapy, anti-psychiatry, Third World camp-following, and belief in the occult. The exaltation of community does not preclude the search for absolute leadership; on the contrary, it may inevitably lead to it.[58]

That other extraordinary Levi from Turin—Primo Levi—also discerned fascism's eternal fascination. Primo Levi was also born into a middle-class assimilated Jewish family (in 1919) and completed a degree in chemistry (stamped "Di razza ebraica"). His extensive knowledge of chemistry, his rudimentary knowledge of German, and sheer luck enabled him to survive a year in Auschwitz.[59] During the *anni di piombo* ("years of lead," that is, right- and left-wing domestic terrorism), Primo Levi courageously wrote:

> Every age has its own Fascism, and we see the warning signs wherever the concentration of power denies citizens the possibility and the means of expressing and acting on their own free will. There are many ways of reaching this point, and not just through the terror of police intimidation, but by denying and distorting information, by undermining systems of justice, by paralyzing the education system, and by spreading in a myriad subtle ways nostalgia for a world where order reigned, and where the security of the privileged few depends on the forced labor and the forced silence of the many.[60]

Nowhere has this been brought to the page with such conciseness, lucidity, and outrage than in Lewis Lapham's October 2005 essay in *Harper's*, "On Message." [61] This contemporary Mark Twain also referred back to Eco's seminal 1995 essay but remarked on how far we had come in actually implementing the more insidious aspects of fascism. It's no longer a case of what we have to do to be fascist, but what we don't have to do. *We don't have to burn any books*. More books today are published than ever before in human history, "but to people who don't know how to read or think, they do as little harm as snowflakes falling on a frozen pond." *We don't have to disturb, terrorize, or plunder the bourgeoisie*. Contemporary Americans are people "accustomed to regarding themselves as functions of a corporation . . . we're blessed with a bourgeoisie that will welcome fascism as gladly as it accepts the rain in April and the sun in June." *We don't have to gag the press or seize the radio stations*. "People trained to the corporate style of thought and movement have no further use for free speech, which is corrupting, overly emotional, reckless, and ill-informed, not calibrated to the time available for television talk or the performance standards of a Super Bowl halftime show." *We don't have to murder the intelligentsia*. "The society is so glutted with easy entertainment that no writer or company of writers is troublesome enough to warrant the compliment of an arrest, or even the courtesy of a sharp blow on the head." It is "an impressive beginning," concludes Lapham, "but we can do better."

Intimately tied to two cities—his native Turin and his adopted Rome—Carlo Levi uncannily saw the modern metropolis as a metaphor for the dark indistinctness of chaos. Just as the free individual and the creative artist had to break free yet retain ties to the primeval mass, the contemporary city dweller had to navigate the labyrinth crafted by modern technology. Just as the ancient labyrinth had been an image of primeval forest, of chaos, and perhaps "even of the soul inhabited by monsters," so modern technology had led to the "exceedingly contradictory and paradoxical" consequence of neither solving nor overcoming the complexities of chaos but merely offering the *techné* of a "rational reconstruction of the irrational," the creation of "a place of loss and fear"; in short, the creation of another—no less fearful—labyrinth.[62]

In an unpublished fragment found among his papers after his death, Levi offered a tantalizing, momentary glimpse of a subterranean life force just beneath the apparent surface image of things in the contemporary metropolis:

> All discourse tends quite quickly to become archeological. . . . Inside the city is a living precious world, not yet created, not fully in existence. . . . At each moment it bobs to the surface, then plunges back into the depths of the objective sea of servitude; it has no language with which to express itself completely. Yet, at the same time, it is not dried out and dead like the stones and the architecture, which the sun of time tinges with a golden, ephemeral light.[63]

After his death from pneumonia in January 1975, Carlo Levi was laid to rest not in his native city of Turin nor his adopted city of Rome but—as he specifically requested—in the small town of Aliano.

On July 1, 1942, as Levi was hiding from the fascists in Florence, he penned the extraordinary essay "Paura della pittura" ("Fear of Painting"). When his friend, the publisher Giulio Einaudi, reprinted *Fear of Freedom* in a new edition in 1964 (it had first appeared in 1946), Levi requested that "Fear of Painting" serve as a new appendix. "Fear of Painting" addresses many of the same issues first raised in *Fear of Freedom*. Here Levi uses painting as a prism through which we can see the problem of freedom in a different light. "Paintings," Levi was to write in *The Watch* (1950), "are mythical landscapes of the soul no matter what subject they represent, and cannot be without intricate, pathless woods, without swamps, without this idle and nocturnal tedium."[64]

More than half a century later Eagleton also saw the relationship between the terror of art and a fear of freedom:

> Aesthetic humanism sets its face against both vacuous formalism and shapeless libertarianism. It sees the work of art as reconciling energy and order, individual and universal, flux and stillness, freedom

and necessity, time and eternity. In doing so, the art-work becomes an allegory of how one might seal the rift in middle-class society between the stasis of its moral and cultural sphere, and the kinesis of its economic and political worlds. Moreover, if the "law" of the artifact is invisibly incarnate in the subject-matter it shapes, then the art-work is politically speaking an image of hegemony rather than coercion. Metaphysically speaking, it is a working model of that reconciliation of love and law which was once known as God. . . . What we need for our security, it appears, is a kind of freedom which could not not exist; and whereas pre-modern civilization found this in God, modernity is forced to substitute for this august solution the far less popular, far less effectual idea of art.[65]

As Giovanna Faleschini-Lerner insists, the distinction between word and symbol is fundamental to Levi's poetics and aesthetics:

For Levi, symbols are abstract. They do not bear a direct relationship with reality—whereas the meaning of all art is precisely the revelation of connections between signs and their referents. In fact, elsewhere Levi says that the purpose of art is to create reality in the moment in which reality is represented. Sign and referent, in other words, must coincide. The problem with modern art (modernism in general, really) for Levi is that it renounces realism, and thus can no longer represent the world, which becomes monstrous and alien to humanity. Hence Levi's insistence on "consenso" as the correspondence of representation and its object through the mediation of the artist who expresses in this formal correspondence his embrace of the object of representation.

Levi's startling condemnation of Picasso and abstract art in "Fear of Painting" is based on this premise: that abstract art reveals the desperate desire to escape from reality. "The Hero is the opposite of Eros," writes Giovanna Faleschini-Lerner,

where Eros is meant as relationality, the capacity to establish a meaningful relationship with reality. "Fear of Painting" is thus a condemnation of modernism and avant-garde as an irresponsible retreat from reality. According to Levi, artistic modernism is a reflection of the crisis of the humanistic philosophical model, a crisis that defines the first half of the twentieth century and that allows for the rise of Fascism. Hence the importance of publishing *Fear of Freedom* and "Fear of Painting" together. Abstractism is a result of the isolation of the individual within the mass, which in turn becomes a tool in the hands of totalitarian leaders. As signs are separated from referents, so the individual is separated from others and from the world. For Levi, all modernism is really abstractism—abstract in the sense of "severed" from reality.[66]

Many years later, Levi returned to this theme in an essay "Riflessioni su Paura della pittura." By 1970, he had concluded that modernism—in its myriad guises—had failed to fulfill the promise of its infinite possibilities. "But this—to give reality, add the category of reality and existence, their names, their form to the aspects of the world—this has always been the nature itself of art. This has been its necessity, its existential value. And this cannot be realized without the conquest and the invention of a unitary and total relationship among all moments of human experience."[67] His conclusion confirms his condemnation of modernism and his affirmation of the value of realism.

For Carlo Levi, fascism—in its failed attempt to embrace and sterilize everything—is forced to realize itself in death. Placing itself at the service of barbarism, the negation of freedom, and the instruments that destroy autonomy and that impose the most stifling conformity and alienation, fascism had thought of itself as the catalyst of history. Instead it proved itself tragically bound by the forces it had unleashed. In making the State an empty but ferocious ideal, it had transformed men and women into dead objects.[68]

Like that first exiled intellectual, Adam—responsible for putting a name on all things—Carlo Levi seeks in *Fear of Freedom* and "Fear of Painting" to put a name on a certain melancholy that ripens into a holy terror, a dumb awe, a trembling before the gods.

He had intuited the divine double bind of modernity: that we must differentiate ourselves from the maternal indistinct chaos in order to be free; but in order to be creative, we must never sever our genealogical ties that bind us to that fertile yet terrifying sacredness.

Notes

1. See, in English, Lawrence Baldassaro, "Paura della libertà: Carlo Levi's Unfinished Preface," *Italica* 72, no. 2 (Summer 1995): 143–54; and David Ward, *Carlo Levi: Gli italiani e la paura della libertà* (Florence: La Nuova Italia, 2002), 49–53; Ward, *Antifascisms: Cultural Politics in Italy, 1943–1946: Benedetto Croce and the Liberals, Carlo Levi and the "Actionists"* (Madison, N.J.: Fairleigh Dickinson University Press, 1996), 157–91. For the initial reaction by the Italian literary establishment, see Paolo Alatri, "Carlo Levi: *Paura della libertà*," *La Repubblica*, March 16, 1947, 3; Leone Bortone, "Carlo Levi: *Paura della libertà*," *Il Ponte* (June 1947): 92–93; Aldo Bizzari, "Un saggio di Carlo Levi," *La Fiera Letteraria*, February 13, 1947, 6–7.
2. Fondazione Carlo Levi, busta 21, fascicolo 755; quoted in Gigliola De Donato and Sergio D'Amaro, *Un torinese al Sud: Carlo Levi. Una biografia* (Milan: Baldini & Castoldi, 2001), 142–43 (my translation).
3. Erich Fromm, *Escape From Freedom* (New York: Rinehart, 1941), reprinted recently as *The Fear of Freedom* (London: Routledge, 2001); Umberto Eco, "Ur-Fascism," *New York Review of Books* 42, no. 11. (June 22, 1995): 12–15, reprinted in a slightly different version as "Ur-Fascism," in *Five Moral Pieces*, trans. Alastair McEwen (New York: Harcourt, 2001), 65–88, and "Il fascismo eterno," in *Cinque scritti morali* (Milan: RCS Libri, 1997), 25–48; Robert O. Paxton, *The Anatomy of Fascism* (New York: Alfred A. Knopf, 2004); Terry Eagleton, *Holy Terror* (Oxford: Oxford University Press, 2005); Lewis Lapham, "On Message," *Harper's*, October 2005, 7–9, available online at http://www.marxmail.org/lapham.htm.
4. For insights into the Jewish culture in Turin, see the first chapter, "Argon," in Primo Levi, *The Periodic Table*, trans. Raymond Rosenthal (New York: Schocken Books, 1984), 3–20; and Rita Levi-Montalcini's memoir, *In Praise of Imperfection*, trans. Luigi Attardi (New York: Basic Books, 1988). For a revisionist challenge to the image of Turin a center of antifascism, see Angelo D'Orsi, *La cultura a Torino tra le due guerre* (Turin: Einaudi, 2000).
5. On the fascinating figure of Piero Gobetti, see his *On Liberal Revolution*, trans. William McCuaig, ed. Nadia Urbinati (New Haven, Conn.: Yale University Press, 2000); Paolo Bagnoli, *L'Eretico Gobetti* (Milan: La Pietra, 1978); Alberto Cabella, *Elogio della libertà* (Turin: Il Punto, 1998); Marco

Gervasoni, *L'Intellettuale come eroe: Piero Gobetti e le culture del Novecento* (Florence: La Nuova Italia, 2000) and the forthcoming work of James Martin, *Piero Gobetti and the Politics of Liberal Revolution* (New York: Palgrave, 2008).

6. On the charismatic Rosselli, see his *Scritti dell'esilio*, ed. Costanzo Casucci, 2 vols. (Turin: Einaudi, 1988, 1992); Nicola Tranfaglia, *Carlo Rosselli. Dall'interventismo a "Giustizia e Libertà"* (Bari: Laterza, 1968); in English, see his *Liberal Socialism*, trans. William McCuaig, ed. Nadia Urbinati (Princeton, N.J.: Princeton University Press, 1994); for the only biography in English, see Stanislao G. Pugliese, *Carlo Rosselli: Socialist Heretic and Antifascist Exile* (Cambridge, Mass.: Harvard University Press, 1999).

7. For a fascinating comparative study of the Italian and American "southern problems," see Enrico Dal Lago and Rick Halpern, eds., *The American South and the Italian Mezzogiorno* (New York: Palgrave, 2002); for an application of Edward Said's "orientalism" thesis to the Mezzogiorno, see Jane Schneider, ed., *Italy's "Southern Question": Orientalism in One Country* (Oxford: Berg, 1998).

8. Giustizia e Libertà, "Schema di Programma," *Quaderni di Giustizia e Libertà* no. 1 (January 1932): 4–8. I am indebted to Professor Frank Rosengarten, who has made the complete run of the *Quaderni* (hereafter cited as *QGL*) available to me.

9. The episode is recounted in Alexander Stille, *Benevolence and Betrayal: Five Italian Jewish Families Under Fascism* (New York: Summit Books, 1991), 99, and Susan Zuccotti, *The Italians and the Holocaust* (New York: Basic Books, 1987), 28.

10. Sion Segre Amar, "Sui 'fatti' di Torino del 1934," *Gli ebrei in Italia durante il fascismo: Quaderni del Centro di Documentazione Ebraica Contemporanea* 2, no. 3 (March 1962): 126.

11. Meir Michaelis, *Mussolini and the Jews: German-Italian Relations and the Jewish Question in Italy, 1922–1945* (Oxford: Oxford University Press, 1978), 57–80.

12. Renzo De Felice, *Storia degli ebrei italiani sotto il fascismo* (Turin: Einaudi, 1993), 147, and Joel Blatt, "The Battle of Turin, 1933–1936: Carlo Rosselli, Giustizia e Libertà, OVRA, and the Origins of Mussolini's Anti-Semitic Campaign," in *Journal of Modern Italian Studies* 1, no. 1 (Fall 1995): 22–57.

13. OVRA report of 20 December 1933, Archivio Centrale dello Stato, Polizia Politica, Busta 114, June 7, 1936.

14. See Blatt, "The Battle of Turin, 1933–1936," 33.

15. See the new edition of *Christ Stopped at Eboli*, trans. Frances Frenaye, intro. Mark Rotella (New York: Farrar, Straus and Giroux, 2006), 3.

16. Ibid., 4.

17. Ibid., 249–50.

18. See especially Fromm, *Escape From Freedom*, but also later books such as

Man For Himself (New York: Rinehart, 1947); *The Sane Society* (New York: Rinehart, 1955); and *The Anatomy of Human Destructiveness* (New York: Holt, Rinehart and Winston, 1973).

19. Rosselli, "Essenza del fascismo," Archivio Giustiza e Libertà, desposited in the Istituto Storico della Resistenza in Toscana, Florence.
20. Rosselli, "Risposta a Giorgio Amendola," *QGL* no. 1 (January 1932): 35.
21. Carlo Levi, "Seconda lettera dall'Italia," *QGL* no. 2 (March 1933): 11; reprinted in *Coraggio dei miti: Scritti contemporanei, 1922–1974*, ed. Gigliola De Donato (Bari: De Donato Editore, 1975), 33–40.
22. Emilio Lussu, "Errico Malatesta," *QGL* no. 5 (December 1932): 37–41.
23. Ferruccio Parri, *Scritti 1915–1975* (Milan: Feltrinelli, 1976), 179.
24. Ferruccio Parri, "Discussione sul Risorgimento," *Giustiza e Libertà* (the weekly newspaper published by the movement), April 26, 1935.
25. Levi, "Il programma dell'Opposizione Comunista," *QGL* no. 4 (September 1932): 49.
26. "La situazione italiana e i compiti del nostro movimento," *QGL*, no. 5 (December 1932): 4.
27. "E. Bianchi" (Carlo Levi), "Sport," *QGL* no. 10 (February 1934): 46–50.
28. Levi, *Christ Stopped at Eboli*, 252.
29. "Lascerei volontieri ad altri l'amaro calice": see Federico Garimberti, "È Fini il mio successore," *America Oggi*, January 27, 2007, 5.
30. See Berlusconi, interview with Boris Johnson and Nicholas Farrell, *The Spectator*, September 11, 2003.
31. Frank Bruni, "Berlusconi, in a Rough Week, Says Only He Can Save Italy," *New York Times*, May 10, 2003.
32. For a further discussion of this episode, see my essay "A Past That Will Not Pass: Fascism, Anti-Fascism, and the Resistance in Italy," in *Fascism, Anti-Fascism and the Resistance in Italy: A Critical Anthology*, ed. Pugliese (Lanham, Md.: Rowman & Littlefield, 2004), 1–22.
33. For two brilliant contemporary analyses, see Paul Ginsborg, *Silvio Berlusconi: Television, Power, and Patrimony* (London: Verso, 2004); and Alexander Stille, *The Sack of Rome: How a Beautiful European Country with a Fabled History and a Storied Culture Was Taken Over by a Man Named Silvio Berlusconi* (New York: Penguin, 2006).
34. Levi, *Christ Stopped at Eboli*, 253.
35. In fact, *Escape From Freedom* was published in Britain as *Fear of Freedom* (London: Paul, Trench, Trubner & Co., 1942; London: Routledge, 2001).
36. Fromm, *Escape From Freedom*, viii.
37. Ibid., 23.
38. Ibid., 134.
39. Ibid., 240.
40. Ibid., 274.
41. Umberto Eco, "Ur-Fascism," in *The New York Review of Books* 42, no. 11. (June 22, 1995): 12–15.

42. On this, see Jeffrey Herf, *Reactionary Modernism: Technology, Culture, and Politics in Weimar and the Third Reich* (Cambridge: Cambridge University Press, 1984).

43. Robert O. Paxton, "The Five Stages of Fascism," *Journal of Modern History* 70, no. 1 (March 1998): 1–23.

44. Robert O. Paxton, *The Anatomy of Fascism*, 9.

45. Ibid., 41, 219.

46. John Dewey, *Freedom and Culture* (New York: Putnam, 1939), 44.

47. Ibid., 58.

48. Henry A. Wallace, "The Danger of American Fascism," *New York Times*, April 9, 1944; reprinted in Wallace, *Democracy Reborn* (New York: Reynal & Hitchcock, 1944), 259.

49. Eagleton, *Holy Terror*, vi.

50. Ibid., 2.

51. Ibid., 115.

52. Ibid., 68.

53. Ibid., 71–72.

54. Ibid., 77.

55. Ibid., 81.

56. Ibid., 82.

57. Susan Sontag, "Fascinating Fascism," *New York Review of Books*, February 6, 1975; reprinted in Sontag, *Under the Sign of Saturn* (New York: Farrar, Straus & Giroux, 1980), 73–105.

58. Ibid., 96.

59. Primo Levi's two extraordinary memoirs, *Se questo è un uomo* (Turin: De Silva, 1947) and *La tregua* (Turin: Einaudi, 1963), published in the United States as *Survival in Auschwitz* and *The Reawakening*, both translated by Stuart Woolf (New York: Summit, 1985) are today acknowledged as masterpieces of Holocaust literature, as is his last work, *I sommersi e i salvati* (Turin: Einaudi, 1986), in English: *The Drowned and the Saved*, trans. Raymond Rosenthal (New York: Summit, 1988).

60. Primo Levi, in *Corriere della Sera*, May 8, 1974; reprinted in *L'asimmetria e la vita*, ed. Marco Belpoliti (Turin: Einaudi, 2002); translated as "The Past We Thought Would Never Return," in Levi, *The Black Hole of Auschwitz*, trans. Sharon Wood (New York: Polity Press, 2005), 34.

61. Lewis Lapham, "On Message," *Harper's*, October 2005, 7–9.

62. Carlo Levi, "The Labyrinth," in *Fleeting Rome*, trans. Antony Shugaar (Chichester: John Wiley & Sons, 2004), 216–17.

63. Carlo Levi, "Fleeting Rome," in *Fleeting Rome*, trans. Antony Shugaar (Chichester: John Wiley & Sons, 2004), 235.

64. Carlo Levi, *The Watch* (South Royalton, Vt.: Steerforth Italia, 1999), 53.

65. Eagleton, *Holy Terror*, 87–88.

66. Giovanna Faleschini-Lerner, private correspondence.

67. Carlo Levi, "Reflessioni su Paura della pittura," in Levi, *Lo specchio*.

Scritti di critica d'arte, ed. Pia Vivarelli (Rome: Donzelli, 2001), 27–29. I am indebted to Professor Faleschini-Lerner for this reference and her translation of the passage cited.

68. Carlo Levi, "Le cartoline della storia," introduction to *Autobiografia del fascismo*, ed. Enzo Nizza (Milan: La Pietra, 1962), vi.

Basic Chronology of Carlo Levi's Life
Sergio D'Amaro

1902
29 *November*. At 12:45 A.M., Carlo Levi is born. He is the son of Ercole
Levi and Annetta Treves; his mother is the sister of the socialist
leader Claudio Treves and Marco Treves, a psychiatrist. Upon learning of the birth, Claudio Treves sends the family a picture postcard
depicting Mazzini.

1915
He paints his first canvas, depicting a dawn and his own home.

c. 1917
He executes his first portrait, inspired by Dürer's *Self-Portrait with Glove*
(see the catalogue *Carlo Levi si ferma a Firenze*, ed. C.L. Ragghianti,
28).

1917
After attending secondary school at the Liceo "Alfieri," he enrolls in the
Department of Medicine at the University of Turin.

1918
November. He meets Piero Gobetti. *Energie Nove* begins publication.

1921
Occupation of the Società di Cultura by Gobetti's group. Levi also takes
part, and speaks jokingly of a "coup d'état."

1922
October/November. While traveling with his brother Riccardo, he visits
Florence, Rome, and Naples. He begins writing for Gobetti's *La Riv-
oluzione Liberale*.

1923

He exhibits a portrait of his father at the Quadriennale in Turin. Gobetti's publishing house is founded. He meets Felice Casorati through Gobetti.

1924

He earns a degree summa cum laude in medicine. He exhibits at the Fourteenth Venice Biennale. The group of *La Rivoluzione Liberale* votes for the Communists during the political elections. He has been romantically involved with Maria Marchesini for some time. At the home of Giacomo Debenedetti he meets Umberto Saba, whom he will see again in Florence during the Nazi occupation.

1924–1928

He works with Professor Micheli at the Medical Clinic of the University of Turin. He does experimental work on liver disease and diseases of the bile ducts. In Paris, he attends postgraduate courses with Professors Bourguignon, Vidal, Besançon, and others.

1925–1926

He performs his military service, first in Florence and then at the Moncenisio. He frequents the Rosselli brothers. He witnesses the attack on Gaetano Salvemini.

1925

First stay in Paris. He has a studio in the Rue de la Convention.
1 November. La Rivoluzione Liberale is obliged to cease publication.
He meets Edoardo Persico, who moved to Turin that year.

1926

16 February. Piero Gobetti dies in Paris.
Levi's family purchases a villa in Alassio. He publishes an article, "Soffici in Venice," in *Il Baretti*. He takes part in the Fifteenth Venice Biennale.

1927

Second stay in Paris. He develops a romantic attachment to Vitia Gourevitch. He meets Mario Andreis and Aldo Garosci. He takes part in the meetings of the *Baretti* in the Via Fabro and talks with Monti, De Rosa, Passerin d'Entrèves, and Brosio. He decides to devote himself completely to painting.

1928

Third stay in Paris. *Il Baretti* ceases publication.

1929

With Nello Rosselli and Riccardo Bauer he founds *La Lotta Politica*. He takes part in the exhibition "Sei Pittori a Torino," with J. Boswell, G. Chessa, N. Galante, F. Menzio, and E. Paulucci. The show travels to Turin (January), Genoa (April–May), and Milan (November).

Carlo Rosselli escapes from the island of Lipari and makes his way to Paris where, in August, the Giustizia e Libertà (Justice and Liberty) movement is founded.

Levi moves his Paris studio to the Rue du Cotentin.

1929–1931

With Mario Andreis he is in charge of the organization of the Turin group, Giustizia e Libertà. He designs stamps and the cover of Lussu's book, *La catena*, with the symbol of Giustizia e Libertà.

1930

He takes part in the Seventeenth Venice Biennale. Second Turinese exhibition of the "Sei Pittori" at the Sala Guglielmi in Turin.

With Menzio and Paulucci, he exhibits at the Bloomsbury Gallery in London, with a presentation by Lionello Venturi.

25 November–5 December. Group exhibition of the Novecento Italiano in Buenos Aires.

He paints *L'Eroe Cinese* (The Chinese hero).

1931

January. He exhibits at the Galleria d'Arte di Roma.

He contributes to the Turin newsletter, *Voci d'Officina*, edited by R. Poli, M. Andreis, A. Garosci, L. Scala, B. Allason, A. Rho, and others. He takes part in the composition of the *Programma rivoluzionario di Giustizia e Libertà* with Carlo Rosselli, Emilio Lussu, Alberto Tarchiani, Gaetano Salvemini, and Francesco Nitti. Many of the members of Giustizia e Libertà also contribute to Einaudi's journal *La Cultura*.

In Rome, along with Paulucci, he begins to work on film sets for the movie studio Cines. He works on the movies *Patatrac* (G. Righelli) and *Ricordo d'Infanzia* (M. Soldati).

He meets with Renato Guttuso.

December. He exhibits with Chessa, Menzio, Paulucci, and Spazzapan at the Paris gallery Jeune Europe with a catalogue presentation by Lionello Venturi.

1931–1932

In Paris, he meets Stravinsky and Prokofiev. He is in close contact with

Garosci, Ferrata, and Luigi Ferrero, regularly meeting them at the restaurant Rouget on the Boulevard St. Michel.

Meetings with Noventa, Alberto Moravia, and Nicola Chiaromonte. He spends time with De Chirico, Severini, and Tozzi.

1932

June. First solo exhibition in Paris at the Jeune Europe gallery.

He takes part in the Eighteenth Venice Biennale. He publishes, in the *Quaderni di Giustizia e Libertà*, his "Seconda lettera dall'Italia" (Second letter from Italy) and "Il concetto di autonomia nel programma di Giustizia e Libertà" (The concept of autonomy in the program of Justice and Liberty).

1932–1933

He serves as an intermediary between Turin and antifascist exiles.

1932–1934

He spends nearly all this time in Paris.

1933

He attends the Paris funeral of his uncle Claudio Treves.

He publishes in the *Quaderni di Giustizia e Libertà* "In morte di Claudio Treves" and "Piero Gobetti e la rivoluzione liberale" (On the death of Claudio Treves and Piero Gobetti and the liberal revolution).

March. He moves to no. 6 Villa Chauvelot, Paris 15.

June. Solo exhibition at the Bonjean gallery.

He is in touch with Unafilm.

1933–1935

He works in the organizational center of Giustizia e Libertà, with Vittorio Foa and Leone Ginzburg.

1934

13 March. He is arrested at Alassio and interned in the prison of Turin for suspected participation in Giustizia e Libertà, in the wake of the arrest of Sion Segre and the escape of Mario Levi to Ponte Tresa (the "Togo affair").

26 April. *La Libertà* publishes an appeal by a number of artists living in Paris (including Léger, Chagall, and Derain) for Levi's release.

9 May. He is released. The Commissione Provinciale per l'Ammonizione e il Confino di Polizia (Provincial Commission for Warning and Police Internment) orders special warning status for two years. His request for the drawings he did in prison is rejected.

He works with Soldati at Lux Film, under the supervision of the musicologist Gatti.

He takes part in a traveling exhibition in the United States.

1934–1935
Long stays in Alassio, alternating with time in Turin.

He continues his relations with Foa and *La Cultura* (Einaudi, Antonicelli, Pavese, Cajumi, et al.), where he signs his work with the pseudonym "Tre Stelle" (Three Stars).

1935
April. He designs the cover for Mario Soldati's book *America Primo Amore.*

15 May. He is arrested in Turin.

23 May. He is questioned by the political police in Turin and subsequently transferred to the prison of Regina Coeli in Rome.

15 July. The Commissione Provinciale di Roma per l'Assegnazione al Confino di Polizia (Provincial Commission of Rome for Assignment to Police Internment) condemns Carlo Levi to three years' confinement, to be served at Grassano (in the province of Matera).

23 July. He submits an appeal to the Commissione di Appello (Appeals Commission).

3 August. He arrives in Grassano. First he stays at the hotel run by L. Prisco, then in a house owned by the Schiavone family. During his period of confinement he paints at least seventy canvases.

20 August. Paola Levi arrives (he is now romantically involved with her, and she will bear him a daughter in 1937), and leaves again on 2 September.

30 August. The prefect of Matera suggests to the minister of the interior that Levi be trasferred to Aliano, to prevent him from receiving packages and friends that might elude censorship.

17 September. His sister Luisa arrives in Grassano.

18 September. He is moved to Aliano. He takes a room at the Albergo Moderno.

23 September. He draws up a list of the people with whom he intends to correspond.

5 October. His sister Luisa leaves for Turin.

20 October. He takes up residence in a house owned by relatives of the archpriest of Aliano.

30 November. He is in Grassano for a week, to finish a few paintings.

1935–1936

He develops a plan for drainage and reclamation, and for prevention of malaria, in the Aliano area.

1936

9 February. Letter to the *questore*, or chief of police, of Matera protesting the prohibition against his practicing medicine.

February–March. He is in Turin following the death of an uncle.

1 May. Inauguration of the exhibition of the Società Promotrice di Belle Arti (Society for the Encouragement of Fine Arts) of Turin. Levi takes part, with three canvases of Lucanian subjects.

20 May. The minister of the interior orders the liberation of all political internees, in commemoration of the proclamation of the Italian Empire.

26 May. Levi leaves for Turin, where he resumes his political activity.

November. Personal show at the Il Milione gallery in Milan, in which he exhibits paintings he did while in political internment.

December. Personal show at the Genova gallery in Genoa, with a catalogue introduction by Giansiro Ferrata.

1937

May. Solo exhibition at the La Cometa gallery in Rome, with a catalogue introduction by Sergio Solmi.

9 June. Assassination of the Rosselli brothers at Bagnoles-sur-l'Orne. Levi paints *Autoritratto con la camicia insanguinata* (Self-portrait with bloody shirt).

November. Designer and set painter in Rome for the film *Pietro Micca.*

December. He exhibits in New York in the "Anthology of Contemporary Italian Painting."

1938

He composes, in Nice and Cannes, a number of short verses in intimist and elegiacal style. Long winter evenings spent in the company of Franco Venturi, Aldo Garosci, and Paolo Vittorelli. He contributes to the weekly *Giustizia e Libertà.*

1939

Obliged to escape to France, he is at La Baule, near St. Nazaire in Brittany, from September to December. Here he writes *Paura della libertà* (*Fear of Freedom*).

1940

He spends time in Cannes and Marseilles. During this period, he refuses to go to the United States, although he could easily have taken advantage of the international visa extended by Roosevelt to all persecuted European intellectuals.

1941

He returns to Italy. In Milan, he meets Ugo La Malfa in order to agree on the terms and means by which the clandestine struggle will be carried on.

1942

He joins the Partito d'Azione (Action Party), heir to Giustizia e Libertà. He writes the essay "Paura della pittura" ("Fear of Painting," later published, in 1948, in Carlo Ludovico Ragghianti's monograph on Levi). He takes up residence in Florence, where he becomes one of the leading figures in the Partito d'Azione. He has a studio in the Piazza Donatello. He meets or spends time with Delfini, Montale, Gadda, Bazlen, Q. Martini, Cancogni, Tobino, Antonicelli, Timpanaro Sr., and P. Santi.

1943

April. He is arrested and conveyed to the Florence prison, Carcere delle Murate, where he remains until 26 July.

September. He is a guest of Eugenio Montale when "the days of misfortune" begin. Montale himself was to welcome many antifascist partisans and members of the Comitato di Liberazione Nazionale (CLN).

December 1943–July 1944. In Fiesole, and later in Florence in the Piazza Pitti, where he continues to live in hiding, he writes *Cristo si è fermato a Eboli* (*Christ Stopped at Eboli*). In this period, he meets Umberto Saba once again, and also meets his daughter Linuccia, who will become his partner until his death.

1943–1944

He executes a number of monotypes on the theme of the war, either as lived or as foreshadowed.

1944

Following the liberation of Florence (11 August), he participates as a representative of the Partito d'Azione to the Comitato Toscano di Liberazione Nazionale.

September. He becomes deputy director of the daily *La Nazione del popolo*, mouthpiece of the CLN.

1943–1945

He serves as a member of the press commission of the CLN and on the commission of architects and technicians for the reconstruction of the historical center of Florence.

1945

24 April. He is named chairman of the commission on urban planning and construction for the committee for the reconstruction of the province of Florence.

June. He moves to Rome, where he works as the director of *L'Italia Libera*, national publication of the Partito d'Azione, until February of 1946.

Einaudi publishes *Cristo si è fermato a Eboli*. The book is translated into various languages and becomes a best-seller in the United States.

1946

The founding manifesto of the Nuova Secessione Artistica Italiana is published: among the signatories are Levi, Birolli, Cassinari, Guttuso, Leoncillo, Morlotti, Pizzinato, Santomaso, Vedova, and Viani.

April. Solo exhibition at the Galleria del Bosco in Turin.

May. He runs as a candidate for the Constituent Assembly, affiliated with the Alleanza Repubblicana (Republican Alliance) party, in the ward of Bari-Foggia and in the ward of Potenza-Matera, where he returns for the first time since his internment. In Basilicata (Lucania), he meets Rocco Scotellaro.

December. Solo exhibition at the Lo Zodiaco gallery in Rome, with a catalogue introduction by Ragghianti.

He begins contributing to *La Stampa*. He publishes *Paura della libertà (Fear of Freedom)*.

1947

May. First American solo exhibition at the Wildenstein Gallery in New York.

December. He is present at the founding conference of the Fronte del Mezzogiorno.

He is a participant in the Movimento per la Pace (Movement for Peace): he meets, among others, Neruda and Curie.

1947–1948

He does a series of satirical cartoons for the daily *L'Italia Socialista*, directed by Garosci.

1948

He exhibits at the Twenty-fourth Biennale, in a hall of his own. The Fronte Nuovo delle Arti triumphs in Venice.

February. Solo exhibition at the L'Obelisco gallery in Rome.

Edizioni U in Florence publishes Ragghianti's monograph on his oeuvre as a painter.

1949
He takes part in the Assise del Mezzogiorno with Amendola, Gatto, and Quasimodo.

1950
He takes part in the Congresso della Resistenza (Congress of the Resistance) in Venice. He publishes *L'orologio* (*The Watch*) with Einaudi.

1951
January. He takes part in the second art exhibition against barbarianism at the Galleria in Rome, organized by the realistic painters Penelope, Guttuso, Mafai, Trombadori, and Socrate, in response to Eisenhower's visit.
He writes a series articles on the flooding of the Polesine.

1951–1952
He travels through Calabria, from Melissa to the Sila, accompanied by Rocco Scotellaro. He also visits Sicily and Sardinia.

1952
March. Solo exhibition at the La Colonna gallery in Milan.

1953
February–March. He exhibits two groups of paintings on Calabrian subjects at the Il Pincio gallery of Rome.
May–June. The magazine *L'Illustrazione Italiana* publishes his article "Contadini di Calabria" (Peasants of Calabria).

1954
He takes part in the Twenty-eighth Venice Biennale, exhibiting no fewer than fifty canvases in his own personal hall, with a catalogue introduction by Garosci.
He joins the group of neorealist painters.
He writes prefaces to J. De Castro, *Geografia della fame* (originally published in Portuguese as *Geografia da fome* [*Geography of Hunger*], Italian edition De Donato) and Rocco Scotellaro, *È fatto giorno* (Mondadori).

1955
March. Personal exhibition with the series *Gli Amanti* (The lovers) at the Il Pincio gallery in Rome, with a catalogue presentation by Italo Calvino.

He takes part in the conference at Matera on Scotellaro.

He travels to the U.S.S.R. and takes his third trip to Sicily.

He exhibits, at the Seventh Quadriennale of Rome, *Lamento per Rocco Scotellaro*.

He serves on a cabinet-level commission for the preservation of the Appian Way.

He publishes *Le parole sono pietre: Tre giornate in Sicilia* (*Words Are Stones: Impressions of Sicily*) with Einaudi.

He writes a preface to Rocco Scotellaro's, *L'uva puttanella* (Laterza).

1956

January. He travels to India.

3 December. He publishes in *Il punto* a "Lettera agli scrittori sovietici" (Letter to Soviet authors).

He publishes *Il futuro ha un cuore antico* (The future has an ancient heart), which later wins the Premio Viareggio.

1956–1957

He publishes a series of essays on art criticism in *L'Illustrazione Italiana*.

1957

Commemoration of Di Vittorio, Dorso, and Salvemini.

17 November. He delivers a speech on unemployment at the Teatro Politeama in Palermo.

He helps with the design of the headstone for Scotellaro's grave.

He writes a preface to C. De Brosses, *Viaggio in Italia. Lettere familiari* (Italian edition of *Lettre familières d'Italie: Lettres écrites d'Italie en 1739 et 1740*), published with Parenti.

1958

May. In the general election, he is a candidate for the Italian senate, as a member of the PSI (Italian Socialist Party), for the ward of Acireale.

He travels to Germany.

He writes a preface to L. Sterne, *La vita e le opinioni di Tristram Shandy, gentiluomo* (Italian edition of *The Life and Opinions of Tristram Shandy, Gentleman*), published with Einaudi.

1959

He travels to China. He publishes *La doppia notte dei tigli* (*The Linden Trees*) with Einaudi.

1960

January. Group exhibition at the Chiurazzi gallery in Rome. The seven canvases that he exhibits mark, according to critics, a watershed in Levi's artistic development.

May. He delivers a speech on employment and development in southern Italy (a keynote address for the conference on work and development in southern Italy held in Palma di Montechiaro).

July. Articles in *ABC* in the section "Parole chiare" on the days of insurrection in Reggio Emilia.

6 August. He delivers a speech at Reggio Emilia in the Piazza della Libertà on the thirtieth anniversary of the deaths of five antifascists (it appears as a preface to Renato Nicolai, *Reggio Emilia, 7 Luglio 1960,* Editori Riuniti).

He writes a preface to Stendhal, *Roma Napoli e Firenze* (Italian edition of *Rome, Naples, et Florence*) published with Parenti. He publishes *Un volto che ci somiglia: Ritratto dell'Italia* with Einaudi.

1961

May. He executes a large oil painting, measuring 18.5 meters by 3.2 meters, for the Lucania Pavilion at the exposition "Italia 61–Mostra dell'Unità d'Italia"

Preface to Pier Paolo Pasolini, *Accattone.* He writes the preface to the catalogue of Renato Guttuso's exhibition in Moscow.

1962

He signs the "Appello dei 12," a document that demands that Italy have nothing to do with atomic war.

April–May. Solo exhibition at the La Nuova Pesa gallery in Rome (works from 1929 to 1934), with a catalogue introduction by Antonio Del Guercio.

Second trip to Sardinia.

He writes a preface to *Autobiografia del fascismo,* edited by Enzo Nizza (La Pietra). He writes a preface to Michele Pantaleone, *Mafia e politica* (Einaudi).

1963

Letters to Alicata and Khruschev.

28 April. He is elected senator in the ward of Civitavecchia as an independent running in the lists of the PCI (Italian Communist Party) and he joins the mixed group. He becomes a member of the Commissione Istruzione Pubblica e Belle Arti (Commission on Public Education and Fine Arts).

21 December. First speech to the Senate, on the Moro government.

Solo exhibition of drawings and monotypes at the La Cavourrina gallery in Turin.

He writes a preface to Ignazio Buttitta, *La peddi nova* (Feltrinelli). He writes a preface to *Notte sull'Europa*, edited by Fernando Etnasi and Roberto Forti (Rome).

1964

He becomes a member of the commission of inquiry for the protection and exploitation of historic, archeological, artistic, and natural resources (Franceschini Commission). He oversees with the Honorable Vedovato the second study group, charged with investigating medieval, modern, and contemporary historic and artistic resources, and develops the report on contemporary art, published in the first volume of the *Atti della Commissione* (Proceedings of the commission)

14 April. Speech to the Senate on cultural resources.

1 August. Speech to the Senate on the vote of confidence in the second Moro government.

He publishes *Tutto il miele è finito* (All the honey is finished) with Einaudi.

1965

He participates in numerous exhibitions commemorating the Resistance.

Between September and October, he exhibits forty-eight works in the historic retrospective "I Sei di Torino," organized by the Galleria Civica d'Arte Moderna (City Gallery of Modern Art) in Turin.

1966

26 October. Speech to the Senate on speculation in housing at Agrigento.

11 November. Speech to the Senate on the Florence flood.

Solo exhibition at the Piemonte Artistico e Culturale gallery in Turin. He exhibits ninety landscape paintings of Alassio.

He writes a preface to the catalogue of Guttuso's exhibition in East Berlin.

1967

May. Solo exhibition show at the Circolo Culturale "Rinascita" in Matera. He exhibits seventy-one works, from 1935 to 1967, on southern Italian subjects.

27 June. Speech to the Senate on the police law.

June. Solo exhibition at the "Pro-Loco" in Nereto (province of Teramo).

He founds, with Paolo Cinanni and others, the Federazione Italiana
  Lavoratori Emigrati e Famiglie (Italian Federation of Emigrant Workers and their Families).
A special supplement of the magazine *Galleria* is published (vol. 17,
  nos. 3–6, May–December), dedicated to Carlo Levi, with numerous
  essays and reminiscences. The supplement also includes previously
  unpublished writings.
He writes a preface to Umberto Saba, *L'amicizia* (Mondadori).

1968
Solo exhibition at the La Nuova Pesa gallery in Rome.
19 May. He is reelected to the Senate from the ward of Velletri in the
  list of the PCI-PSIUP (Italian Communist Party and Italian Socialist
  Party of Proletarian Unity). He forms part of the parliamentary group
  of the Independent Left. He becomes a member of the Commission
  on Foreign Affairs.

1969
May. Solo exhibitions at the La Barcaccia gallery in Rome (where he was
  to show his work often in the years that follow) and in Montecatini.
11 August. Speech to the Senate on the crisis of the center-left.

1970
7 April. Speech to the Senate on the Rumor government.
September. In the context of the second edition of the *Incontri Silani*,
  an extensive anthological exhibition is organized by M. De Micheli
  at Lorica (Sila) with works relating to southern Italy.

1971
January. Retrospective exhibition at the La Gradiva gallery in Florence.
October. Solo exhibition at the La Noce gallery in Rome featuring
  graphic works.

1973
28 January. He suffers a detached retina, and undergoes two operations
  at the San Domenico hospital of Rome. He executes, in a temporary
  state of blindness, 140 drawings, and writes, with the help of a special
  easel, a text that will be published, after his death, as *Quaderno a
  cancelli* (Einaudi).

1974
March. He is commissioned, along with Cagli and Guttuso, by General
  Beolchini to execute three artworks in commemoration of the massa-
  cre of the Ardeatine Caves. Cagli illustrates the oppression, Guttuso

the massacre, and Levi the liberation. The artworks are then donated to the monumental complex on the 25 March anniversary.

September. Solo exhibition at the Palazzo Te in Mantua. This is the first great retrospective exhibition, with some 200 works, from 1922 to 1974, and it enjoys great interest and attention from critics and the public. At the conclusion of the show, a round table is held with the participation of Attardi, Pasolini, Soldati, and Del Guercio on the topic of "Literary Influences and Civil Engagement in the Pictorial Career of Carlo Levi."

December. Between the 7th and the 10th of this month he makes his last visit to Basilicata (Lucania), presenting a portfolio of seven lithographic prints inspired by *Cristo si è fermato a Eboli*, published by Editore Esposito of Turin.

23 December. He is admitted to hospital at the Policlinico Umberto I, in Rome.

He writes a preface to Rocco Scotellaro, *Uno si distrae al bivio* (Laterza) and a preface to Paolo Cinanni, *Emigrazione e unità operaria* (Feltrinelli).

1975

January. He dies after several days in a coma. He is buried in Aliano.

The "Persiana" gallery in Palermo exhibits his last work, *Apollo and Daphne*, executed on a goat-skin drum the day before he is admitted to hospital.

Coraggio dei Miti: Scritti contemporanei 1922–1974 (The courage of the meek: Contemporary writings, 1922–1974), an anthology of writings is published posthumously, edited by Gigliola De Donato.

Fear of Freedom

Nudo maschile (Nude male, 1935)

The sacred: the most ambiguous, deep-seated, double-edged of all feelings and senses, worm and eagle alike; a continuous dark denial of freedom and art, and—conversely—a continuous creation of art and freedom.

1 / Ab Jove Principium

b Jove principium—everything begins with Jupiter. And we too must begin there, at this non-existent point from which all things are born. Our Jupiter, however, we need not seek in the skies, but where he is wont to stay, in places most dark and earthly, in the maternal dampness of the deep. He is more akin to the worm than to the eagle; but soon enough, he will find his own heraldic eagles, and extol them above every badge or emblem, for only thus will he avoid being devoured, once and for all, by the true eagles of the heavens.

Beyond metaphors, we cannot grasp anything human, unless we start from the feel of *the sacred*: the most ambiguous, deep-seated, double-edged of all feelings and senses, worm and eagle alike; a continuous dark denial of freedom and art, and—conversely—a continuous creation of art and freedom. And again, we cannot understand anything social, unless we start from the meanings of *religion*, this disrespectful heir of things sacred.

What is the process of every religion? To change the *sacred* into the *sacrificial*: to deprive it of its main feature—inexpressibility—by transforming it into deeds and words; to create the ritual out of the mythical; to substitute a sacramental bird for a shapeless turgidity, and marriage for desire; to turn sacred suicide into consecrated slaughter. Religion is relation and relegation. Relegation of a god into a web of formulas, conjurations, invocations, prayers, so that he may not, as is his way, elude us. Sacredness, the very appearance

of terror, shapes itself into law, in order to escape its own self. Pure
anarchy becomes pure tyranny. Man, as a free being, is thus bound
by the selfsame bonds of the sacred, and relegated into a common reciprocal nexus before the deity. There is no rabble without
a king, there are no masses without God. It may be false to claim
that every society grows out of a religious tie; but it is certainly
true that every monarchy is religious. Every king, great or small,
every petty prince and clan chieftain is a sacred majesty: a being
divinely ambiguous, having no true name, except a name symbolic
and heraldic (a number); a being that lives hidden or perhaps may
not live at all; a being the less existent the more it appears to be.
With good reason the most ancient kings—true kings—were beasts
or indeterminate powers of nature; and thus China was ruled by
dragon-kings, by tiger-kings, by demon-kings,—and Egypt, by dog-
faced and falcon-headed royal gods.

The nearer the formless sense of sacredness swims up to the
surface of men's consciousness, the less certain, the more earthly
and manifold are the religious shapes into which it flows and ends.
The deeper the sacred sinks into our inner recesses, the higher the
gods soar into the cloudless sky; and when the sacred in ourselves
is reduced to a disappearing center, to a single point, fiery but extremely remote—then the One God hides beyond the clouds, out
of time, out of space, shrouded in total transcendence. But when
even this vanishing point is forgotten, and the mass grows into
person, God himself loses existence, while the blue skies of day
and the black skies of night cease to watch us like open eyes and
change into fields of serene contemplation, or into wastes tempes-
tuously human, aerial mirrors of the soul.

So, too, the kings and the idols. In times of sacred lore they must
be monsters, stones and trees, and ambiguous terrors of darkness;
in times when religion prevails, they are shepherds, patricians, animals, and thereafter monarchs and images—until the day when
a red Phrygian cap[1] on the head of a Louis crowns constitutional

---

1. A symbol of freedom, the Phrygian cap was adopted by the French Revolution-
aries and is worn by the icon of France, Marianne.

kings, dead kings, worshipped guillotines. But in the short interludes of liberty the kings are forgotten, the idols entombed. These
interludes, like the others (needless to say), do not form an historical progression: they are subjective, they coexist. Everybody is born
from chaos, and to chaos may revert; every man leaves the mass in a
process of differentiation, and in this shapeless mass may lose himself again. But the only vivid moments in an individual life, the only
periods of higher culture in history are those in which the two contrary processes of differentiation and undifferentiation find a common point of equilibrium and are coexistent in the creative act.

What is undifferentiation and how is it related to sacredness?
The myth of creation out of chaos is truly full of sense. There is
a primeval indistinctness, common to all men, flowing in eternity,
inherent to every aspect of the world, spirit of every being in the
world, memory of all time of the world. All individuals start from
it, urged by an obscure freedom to break loose and gain their own
individual forms, and perpetually drawn back by an obscure necessity and compelled to merge again in this same indistinction.
This twofold endeavor stretches from one death to another: from
prenatal chaos to the natural fading away and extinction. But only
a total detachment from this everlasting indefinite flow, only a void
and egoistic reasoning, only the abstraction of liberty are really and
truly death—as are their opposites: complete lack of self-differen-
tiation, mystic brutish darkness, the bondage of the inexpressible.

The flow of indistinction is *nature* itself, obscure beyond ut-
terance, whose sighs are earthquakes and volcanoes, storms and
constellations—and the unerring unconsciousness of the insect.
Action, on the contrary, is the outcome of complete differentiation:
the individual, severed from the whole, moves on to find his own
shape, and his motion has a meaning only to himself. And again,
action must be distinguished from *achievement*, which results from
creative human activity, and blends at the very same moment individual riches and the treasures of universality—differentiation and
undifferentiation: an activity most individual when soaring above
the individuals, and most universal when intensely singular; born
of freedom and necessity at once: understood by all men through

man's common indistinct nature; transcending everyone, inasmuch as every man is a distinct, single self; but shared by everyone in the free process of individuation and consciousness.

The feeling of a transcendent indistinctness and the terror of it, the dread of indetermination which dwells in those who are in the very act of giving birth to themselves, of severing themselves from the mass—this is the *sacred*.

The way of *religion* is to substitute that which is undifferentiated and inexpressible with concrete images and symbols—so that the sacred may be cast out of our consciousness and replaced by finite, and therefore liberating, objects. That which is common to man and wolf is, through sheer indistinction, a boundless terror—until a totemic image turns it into bearable worship. That which is common to man and man is a mysterious original sin never committed, the transgression of a limit, of all limits, and the agony of the unlimited; until a god man comes to free us, by substituting himself for sin, by burdening himself with sin.

Religion is therefore, thus considered, a means in the process of individuation; but a means which, in order to liberate the spirit from the terrifying feeling of transcendency, tends to replace it by visible symbols, by *idols*.

Man does not stand alone before the sky and before his own self. Facing the "I" there is the *other*—all the others, mankind. Every human relation, before it becomes free, must be sacred and religious—for relationship is possible only through the "I" being also the "other," to the point of identity. Closed in himself, the individual tends to separate and live an autonomous life: contact with others is allowed only through that which is common to all, only through the undifferentiated, whose perennial presence renders comprehensible every differentiation. Truly human intercourse, therefore, is always a return to the origins, and that is where shyness and bashfulness arise. The fear of the woman is a sacred horror, for in the act of love every personal memory is blurred—drowned in the universal indistinct memory of the waters of Chaos.

Each truly human relationship breeds, thus, the sense of sacredness, every temporary liberation must be religious in character, must mean the substitution of man by his own symbol, by the idol of his own person. Such is the origin of personal names, family names, coats of arms and banners. A man not free enough to establish communications with his fellows without getting lost, will choose, instead of the actual human intercourse, a purely symbolic relationship, enabling him to remain within himself; and even of his own self each man makes an idol, for fear of reaching, through intimate exploration, those mysterious depths where each self melts away.

That which holds true of the intercourse between individual men, applies equally to the relations of man, society and the state: not only because they, too, are human relationships, but also because society and the state, to those men who do not perceive them as embodiments of their own freedom, must appear as towering giants above understanding. The farther the state is removed from each individual, the mightier it grows in boundless leviathanic complexity, the more it breeds an all-pervasive sense of sacredness. And to relieve us from this sacred horror, society and the state must change into gods.

In the first social nucleus, in the primitive state of the clan, the father is the god. His deification suppresses every truly human intercourse with his kinsmen. He stays in his tent, his appearances are unfrequent; he has the power of blessing and cursing, and his is the right to kill—a right of heroes, not of men. Every attempt to enter into closer relationship with the father appears both anarchical and atheistic, and incest is therefore abominable. Incest deprives Lot of his divine authority, for—his ways being entirely those of nature—he cannot, like Jupiter, change into a bull, a cloud, a golden rain for his miraculous embraces of women. The greatest political offence is that of Ham, son of Noah, who discovers his father's nakedness, because he wants to see his father as a human being.[2] Ambiguity—the transition from the real father to the image of the father-god, and the feeling of profanation in seeing the former through the latter—this is the chief origin of the father-complexes.

---

2. Genesis 9.18–27.

(As for the mother-complexes—whose mechanism is sometimes the same—conditions seem to be entirely reversed: mother and son continue almost physically to be one and the same; the attempted severance and glorification do not succeed, and the complex results from this failure.)

The deification of the father (and the complexes that ensue) last as long as the son's infancy, until the son, peering into himself, perceives himself equal to the father, entirely a man. The deification of the state (and the resulting servitude) will last as long as social infancy, until each man examines his own self and finds in his own complexity the entire structure of the state, and in his own freedom—the necessity of the state. The act of Noah's son is therefore a real sacrilege and political offence—Ham being still in his infancy and not yet seeking in his self the father and the state, but viewing them as gods and himself as son and slave: a rebellious son and slave, not a man free from bondage.

Thus, the state-idol marks at once the need of true human relations and the incapacity to establish them freely; it denotes both the sacred nature of these relations and the inability to differentiate them without drying them up and above all, it is the sign of man's dread of man. This terror of self forms the deepest-rooted of all idolatries, for its fount is ever present, and the most monstrous of all, for it is entirely human. But this idolatry presupposes the sense of an absolute identity of men, and the fear of not being distinguished as *persons*: the sense of a *mass*, of a shapeless humanity, where every individual limit is arbitrary, because the individuals are not really defined. Its opposite is to be found in abstract individualism, wherein every sense of community is lost, while the state, far from being deified, does not even exist, because *passions* are non-existent. This atheism is no less deadly than the idolatry mentioned above. It is useless to be free *from* passions: we ought to be free *in* our passions. For passion is the place where each individual meets the undifferentiated universe; it is the fecundity of sleep everlasting, the eternal return to earlier indistinction—and the problem is to remain ourselves, to retain freedom, in this necessary return.

Abstract individualism, flight from passion, inability to sleep, are nothing but barrenness. But dread of passion, fear of sleeping, the feel of the darkness we are made of, the horror of night's shadow without light—this is the black religion of the state. And, as no Faustian deed is either dream or passion—so, too, none of the thousand cries calling a people to "wake up" can free them from the weight of their slumber, and from the monsters they adore. Only the process of inner maturation will turn the totemic beast, the intangible father, the sacred majesty into the lovely adornments of the past; and then, the temples of Mars, of Vesta, of Janus, and the ceremonial antiquities of England, will remind adult nations that they, too, were infants in days of yore. Good care will be taken, then, of the memories and the myths, which will survive in customs and figures of speech—but so remote as to become incomprehensible. Every word we speak is saturated with religions past and spent; A flight of birds stirs us, because in a faraway time (faraway, though not by-gone) it used to be an omen.

This is true on a personal level as well as on the level of history: that which has been may return once more, that which has been hidden deep may crop out on the surface of our consciousness— like the sands which appear again with the turn of the tide.

Il pastore con l'agnello sul collo (Shepherd with lamb around his shoulders, 1936)

Sacrifice: Without the awareness of this dark necessity, which makes every god true, every servitude willing, every victim sacred; which indissolubly binds the lord and the slave, the king and the prisoner, the banner and exile; without this sense of religious limitation which drives the world on its adored and blood-stained ways, history would be incomprehensible.

2 / Sacrifice

Religion's peculiar process, as we have said, is to change the sacred into the sacrificial, to transform suicide into consecrated slaughter, and anarchy into tyranny. There is no religion without sacrifice: the two terms may be considered altogether equivalent, (even though sacrifice is only a part, an insuppressible modality of religion), for sacrifice denotes a sacred act as well as the killing of the sacred. This primordial necessity, present at every initial phase of religion, cannot be understood when judged by the standards of practical, juridical, contractual reasoning. Tame religions, remote from their origins, no longer sacrifice; they make offerings. Only those who are free from a god can turn to him as to an equal, asking for his gifts and giving to him in exchange. In Lucania,[1] during the procession of the rustic, black-faced Madonna, people throw grain upon her, thus reminding an avaricious earth to grant us another harvest—and also as a due tribute, like those gifts of wheat, animals and eggs, which are brought to the lord of the place whenever one enters his mansion. An infinite number of candles are being lit all over the world, before the images of the saints, that they may bear in mind our needs, and by the flaming lights keep memory of our souls. If formerly such acts were sacrifices, by now they have

---

1. Lucania was the "Romanized" name given by the fascists to the region of Basilicata, where Levi spent a year in *confino* (domestic exile); from that experience came his book *Christ Stopped at Eboli*.

lost their ancient significance, retaining only its shadow and becoming mere human gestures of gratitude, repayment and good omen, even though they are aimed not at humans, but at the likeness of gods. Even the usual meaning of the word sacrifice, denoting voluntary loss, renouncement, detachment, differs in part from its original meaning. Sacrifice is a detachment, a severance, but a bloody severance; it is an act of death, accomplished in order to gain life: it is a religious operation. In the place of sacred indistinction, religion offers us a name and a divine shape, which prevent us from losing ourselves in sacredness, which keep us from suicide and anarchy, which grant us the privilege of living. But this repellent sacredness exerts nevertheless an irresistible attraction; the divine and adored shape, by the very act of adoration, loses its outlines and efficacy and fades into that indistinction from which it originated. In order that the god may live, severance from the sacred must actually take place; the god himself must be not only created and worshiped, but hated and killed: Only the sacramental slaying of the god allows the god to exist: the less he merges with ourselves, but stays aloof and strange and foreign, the greater is his reality. And to make him such, there is no other means than to kill him according to a rite. That is why, whenever a god appears in human guise, it is always in the guise of a stranger, an alien traveler, someone out of another world. Therefore, strangers are gods for those people to whom they reveal themselves for the first time. And therefore, the guest is sacred and cannot be asked his name; while the enemy, the foreigner, is sacred too, but in the opposite sense, and must be killed. *Hostis* and *hostia*[2] are one and the same. Everything is ambiguous in such acts, for that relation with sacredness which brings them forth is ambiguity itself. Here love and hatred, communion and death, do truly coincide, or give birth to one another. In order not to melt away in mystic fusion with the sacred, in order not to die in God, there must be either the freedom of a completed person, or else another death, the death of the god himself, or of the object deified. None of these two ends may stand without the other: without previous suicide, this death has no

---

2. "Enemy" and "host."

efficacy and shrinks to an empty ritual act. Idols are the offspring of a fearful attraction: conversely, an idol can be real only through the relationship of an adoring estrangement. Separation, denial and killing—these are truly the acts which breed the reality of a god. Liberating symbol of an elusive, illimitable reality, the deity has a power of its own inasmuch as it is limited and limitable, and can be denied. The sacrifice of the god (or of a substitute) is at once the affirmation of his existence and the testimony of his reality. The world of rites estranges the incumbent reality. The world of rites estranges the incumbent sacredness, and, conversely, turns sacred everything alien and strange. Every alienation is idol-worship, and there is no idolatry without alienation. In this sense, the victim is always the god, and the god always the victim. Therefore, the agony of the most obscure and tremendous human sin, perhaps the only human sin, the sin of origin, the severance from the formless, the fall into separation, could be redeemed, in the realm of religion, only by the ritual killing of the truest of gods, of the most human of men, of the only one to whom nothing was alien and nothing sacred, for in him, the divine and the human coexisting, there was no original sin.

Thus, the process of sacrifice and that of religion are one and the same—they are both acts of alienation. Therefore, the victim must share the nature of the idol, thus enabling the idol to become estranged and to draw life from this estrangement; or else, the victim must be of the opposite nature, of a nature alien to the idol, and for this very reason consecrated. But always remaining the image of an awe-inspiring communion and the point where each individual loses his limit, the idol—be it a stone or a tree, an animal or a monster, a father, a king or a god—always completely unites with the individual adorer; and therefore, the true sacrifice, the true act of denial of this unity, shall be the alienation of man himself, or of a part of him. Hence the common meaning of the word sacrifice as renouncement, even outside its religious acceptation; and of course there is no religion without renouncement. Something of the sacrificer, a thing which is the sacrificer, something of the idol and which is the idol, has to be voluntarily estranged and destroyed. Only such religious mutilation allows men to live. A mutilation which may consist of a mere obstacle or restriction, or of the loss of a human function or activity, leading even to the point of detachment from earthly goods, of seclusion in the desert. To gods of fecundity and generation are dedicated sacred virgins, or on the contrary—orgiastic mysteries: opposite sacrifices, but of an identical nature. This is the magic origin of vows, of interdictions, of prohibitions which ban certain acts, certain foods, and forbid sexual contacts with women made sacred by pregnancy or by recent delivery. And this is why certain parts of the body become sacred, unmentionable, shameful, and have to be hidden. Something of man must of necessity become strange to man, for the sake of a new life which starts and develops in accordance with religious initiation; something of man must be renounced, expelled, chased out, cut off, to make this life possible. Such is one of the meanings of circumcision, this concrete and localized anticipation of the crucifixion.

So that the god may live, man—in every idolatry—must become estranged from his own self, and victim unto himself; for the god is not God, and man is not yet man. To the deities of nature, bred by the terror of woods, by the mystery of harvests, by physical communion with animals, belong the sacrifice of bullocks and kids, of fruits and crops and firstlings. To the fires of heaven respond the votive fires of forests, and the birth-giving floods are matched by immersions in water, by lustral washings—innocuous symbols of mortal surrenders. But wherever human fright has engendered an idol, the victim shall be human: if not actually a human, at least a symbol of man. Where we have a tribe, and the tribesman is uncertain whether to leave animality or enter it again, sacred animals and men are slain together before beast-like and ambiguous idols: the werewolf issues forth by night in search of victims, and cannibalism is religion. Immortal Minotaurs are nourished forever, in labyrinths and outside labyrinths, upon the flesh of Athenian maidens. Giants and monsters and sphinxes are always awaiting a Theseus, an Hercules, an Oedipus, these liberators from physical uncertainty, these destroyers of double-faced idols and founders of religions preponderantly human. Every wood, every lake, every piece of land holds its feudal dragon, which preys upon men, maids and peasants: and the knight-errant who slays them only substitutes one dynasty for another. Paternal deities, like Saturn, devour their children, and children consummate to all eternity, in their wishes and their actions, the sacrifice of the father. The kings, having put off the vesture of dragons, continue to feed in a religious sense upon their subjects; regicide, it its turn, consecrates the kings.

Every primitive clan, ruled by deified patriarchs, and consequently every patrician state, rests upon sacrifice. In these states, the stranger is sacred; *adversus hostem aeterna auctoritas esto*.[3] But the son himself must be made a stranger: Esau is dispossessed, Ishmael chased away, both necessary victims, and there dies Iphigenia. The first born must be immolated; and they are immolated, as long as the law of the heroes endures; they are carried by their godlike fathers to the high places where blood must flow. And this occurs until Abram bows to a greater and remoter god, and becomes Abraham, a mere human father, divested of any divine attribute, a priest to the universal deity. Then, naturally, the knife falls from his hand, and a ram is substituted for the first-born son: because the new god is no longer the deity of a clan, of a tribe, or of the *patres*, but a true God. Furthermore, such a God being absolutely transcendent and having nothing in common with man, human sacrifice becomes utterly impossible: there remain only crude memories of a former religion of blood, the lamb and circumcision, which is symbolic (this is its secondary meaning) of the slaughter of the first born.

In each of its more complex forms, whenever it is not built upon freedom or made subservient to other ideals, but is considered as a deity in itself, as an idol requiring adoration, the state—like the divinised clan, or tribe, or patriciate—can live only on human sacrifice. Although the ancient prisoner, crowned with flowers or bound in chains, is slain no more upon the altar, the religion of the state requires, in sacrificial form, the renouncement, surrender and death of something human. Without self-mutilation man cannot make a god out of his own capacity for human relations, that

---

3. Usually rendered as "to the enemy no quarter," from Table III of the Roman Law of XIII Tables.

is—out of his ability to shape the state; nor can he free himself religiously from the dread of these relations, from the anxiety of belonging to an indistinct mass. On the individual level, the necessary sacrifice is to renounce autonomy, to accept an infinite series of interdictions and observances, to perceive as justly inaccessible the functions of the state, and to sense as irreverent any desire of grasping them, of sharing in any way the so-called "exercise of sovereignty." The *secret of state* truly becomes the secret of a temple: the layman dare not approach it. If man's power of ruling himself is to be turned into an idol, the very manhood of man must be ceaselessly rejected and expelled as a thing sacred, unmentionable, disgraceful.

On the social level, the necessary sacrifice must be the mutilation of a part of society. A group, a class, a nation must be forcibly driven out, treated as enemies, turned into strangers, so that they may become the god's witnesses and victims. And conversely, the strangers are sacred and must die, while warriors become sacrificers, to be sacrificed in their turn.

Without the awareness of this dark necessity, which makes every god true, every servitude willing, every victim sacred; which indissolubly binds the lord and the slave, the king and the prisoner, the banner and exile; without this sense of religious limitation which drives the world on its adored and blood-stained ways, history would be incomprehensible. Joseph de Maistre, to prove the providential nature of war, uses for arguments the impossibility of explaining it by human motives, its lack of proportion, its futility and unreasonableness. Tested by a purely rationalistic examination, not war alone appears impossible, but slavery as well, and privilege, and wealth, and kingship itself, and almost every historical institution. History becomes meaningless, or an arcane mystery,

. . . which Fate impels by dark enchantment upon its ways,[4]

---

4. "Lo spinge il Fato con oscuro incanto per le sue vie." This may be Levi's slightly mistaken memory from the *Poesie* of Tommaso Campanella (1568–1639): "Lo guida il Fato con occulto incanto / per la gran vita."

or a chaotic mix-up, where the sorcerer may search, if he will, for magic relations of numbers and events; or an absurd adventure of an eternal deceit by priests and tyrants, to which only the light of reason can put an end, by starting a new age of fully explained truth. In truth, the light of reason cannot illuminate this darkness, but only burn these idols and turn them into barren cinders. Beneath this purificatory aridity, darkness will continue to dwell in us, more fathomless and sombre than before. At the beginning of time—so we are told—there was a forest upon the face of the earth. This same primeval forest—shapeless and full of seeds and terrors, hiding in its blackness the features of every face—we bear in ourselves; from it began our earthly journey; and again we find it in the middle of the way, with all its fear; youthful woodland of unlimited powers. Outside liberty, outside creative freedom, every activity, every definition of this infinite potency is but a limitation, a distress, an endless pain, and a sense of irretrievable loss—because every religion is sacrifice and surrender. The first men, according to myth, wandered through boundless woods until they stopped in *certain* places, loved *certain* women and worshiped *certain* gods. And even now, man wanders through an eternal forest, in search of an external certainty; a certainty whose price is servitude and death.

Ritratto di Paola (Portrait of Paola, 1936)

Love is not only the elementary human relationship, the first discovery of the world, the touchstone of liberty, it is also procreation, family, and therefore society and state.

3 / Love Sacred and Profane

Nor may I listen to him who reasons not upon my death.[1]

O
ut of the forest, into the bright light bestowed by a smile of eyes benign—what mortal mood is this, what bitter sense of death? Why does death alone seem company to love, why must the world be fled, and why the chains and the renouncement? To romantic lovers, whose love despairs of anything but mystic fusion, death is the one attainment left for love; it is the blackness of the woods returning, filled with uncertain spasms and distant tremors, and the remote fanfare of the king's hunt. Eternal night without a shape or shore, such is love's own and sacred indistinction: and the beloved face is of the shades of night. For total fusion knows no freedom, will, or gods—only the blind compulsion of deep primeval darkness.

Of another death speaks the humanistic poet, a willing death, a sacrifice, a servitude of love. No more fears of darkness, nor blowing winds of hell: but waters clear, green meadows, and light of days serene. Though even here, in the shades of laurels, a death lies hidden, like a snake amid flowers and grass.

It was woman, indeed, who brought the world out of the black northern forests, peopled by monsters and sullen hierarchies. The damsel had waited for many a century upon her reef, guarded by feudal dragons, pining for the bold warrior who would come and

---

1. "Nè mi lece ascoltar chi non ragiona della mia morte" (Francesco Petrarca [1304–1374], *Canzoniere*, 1372–74).

break her chains: him, in turn, she made a free man. Troubadours
of Provençe and poets of the *Dolce Stil Nuovo*, the sweet new style,
had placed her on the altars, the star and goddess of their rhymes:
but the burden of their songs was the human and the free, and
not the divine. Barbarous male gods gave way before the smiling
Grace: the tongues were loosened and freed from religious reverence, changing their accents and sounds. Femininity's advent had
given the world a new dimension, a perspective which renovated
thought and syntax, language and painting. The greatest of revolutions was flourishing, like all revolutions, under a benign female
deity. Europe returned to womanhood; and the deity's signs were,
in truth, nothing but memories from the former days of feudal
gods. Free courts of love were superseding the cruel courts of lords,
and retaining solely their name and ceremonial; and it is singular
that "courtship," "courting," "courtesy," derive from the usages of
male and heroic times. The sacred hierarchies of vassalage come to
an end when amorous vassalage is chosen. The inarticulate yell of
hunter-kings gives way to feminine speech and human sweetness.
Who could

> For such a wild and barbarous delight
> Forsake the ladies' pleasurable light?[2]

Thereafter, even the memory vanishes of the old gods, and love
profane runs free and sensual in the cities and through the fields,
where the priest of Varlungo, amid chestnuts and onions new, lies
with fair Monna Belcolore.[3] Free are the tongues, not hidden any
more in the obscurity of sacred Latin; free the pursuits of commerce, no longer shameful nor forbidden, but open now to every
Christian; free are the arts and crafts from Byzantine indifference;
free, the relations between men, from symbols, hierarchies and

---

2. Per una sì selvaggia dilettanza
    lasciar le donne a lor gaia sembianza?
    (Dante Alighieri, *Rime*)
3. Levi is here refering to scenes from Giovanni Boccaccio's *Decameron*.

serfdom. And man felt evermore inclined to a personal separate life, to a world impelled by interests and ambitions, resting entirely upon earth, and without gods. However, after the first happy flowering of a creative and impassioned liberty, Italian society broke up into a thousand distinct atoms, partaking no more in the sacred community, but intent with barren appetite of life, upon the merchant's endeavors, the interests of cold reason and the exercise of love. Thence, an impression of void and of peril—and also, from too much liberty, a sense of precariousness and the dread of happiness itself. From these vague and human fears new religions were taking shape—be it that the new lords and masters were reasserting the sacred nature of their strength, or that men of letters and artists were idolizing beauty, so that Giotto and Boccaccio, the most free of spirits, already show the first Latin signs of the coming academies. And man, who had found himself again, himself and his woman, feels the need of excluding her, once more, and of making her a goddess—for the burden of an uncertain liberty weighs upon him. No more a generical goddess of womanhood, Beatrix of freedom and felicity; but a particular divinity, with a name all her own, with her own eyes and hair and face. And, being a deity, she is a stranger and enemy:

So fierce was she, this enemy of mine,
And her I saw, her very heart wounded.[4]

Not freedom any more, but religion is now the basis for relationship with the adored enemy, and her we owe the sacrifice of self. This is the way to servitude of love, a willing servitude in the beginning:

Then did I wander, when the ancient gates
Of liberty were shut and locked before me

---

4. "Era si forte la nemica mia e lei vid' io ferita in mezzo 'l core" (Petrarca, *Canzoniere*).

. . . .
Free at the start upon the path of sorrow
Yet now, alas, in bondage to another
Must go my soul, which sinned only once.[5]

There is an initial sin—idolatry. But this sin once accepted, the
servitude and death which ensue are only natural, for they alone
confirm Laura's divinity, while giving truth and certainty to love. It
is a wandering, a meandering through labyrinths, a failure to recognize one's own face, a renouncement of world and life, a continuous
self-offering, a will to die, which save, however, both the idol and
the believer, and which become eternal law and sacred scripture to
the new religion of love. Without such religion, the thousand rites
and interdictions, the spell of servitude and enchantment, would
have no meaning—and they have none, indeed, in the unspeakable
vortex of sacred love, and none in the pure sensuousness of love
profane, and none in free love's creative comprehension. Weariness
of liberty, unsatisfied senses, fear of the indistinctness of human
communion generate the religion of love. And despite the tears and
the wailing, sacrifice seems a lesser evil than the peril of freedom
in the midst of passion:

Sighing for that which never would return
I said: The burden and the chains of serfdom
Were sweeter than this wandering alone.[6]

---

5. Allora errai quando l'antica strada
   di libertà mi fu precisa e tolta

   . . . .
   allor corse al suo mal libera e sciolta
   ora a posta d'altrui convien che vada
   l'anima, che peccò solo una volta
   (Petrarca, *Canzoniere*)
6. Onde più volte sospirando indietro
   dissi: Ohimè! il giogo e le catene e i ceppi
   eran più dolci che l'andare sciolto.
   (Petrarca, *Canzoniere*)

Petrarca, this greater Cézanne, under the same skies of Provençe, was feeling and summing up the days of liberty gone by and the needs of the new religion: needs of the inmost soul, entirely human terrors, idolatrous quest of salvation.

This historical experience, which we find manifesting itself throughout the centuries and made eternal in art, is equal to the single experience of every man in its various phases, and in the various aspects of each phase. Sacred love, in its limitless power, is anarchy and does not allow any act, but solely a need, indefinite and lethal: such love cannot turn to any particular woman, but only dwell in its own self, in this chaotic oneness from which it proceeds and to which it tends to return. This unbounded potency is impotence. Here man is panting to be one with woman, with all women, in the entirety of an undifferentiated sexuality, in the complete surrender of fusion: the lover is unable to tell himself from his love or to set amorous bounds to the person beloved. And therefore, the gods of this terror must be themselves sexually indeterminate and double, or conversely—excessively male and female. Hence, in the most ancient mythologies, hermaphrodite and mutable deities coexist with other gods, consisting entirely of sex, erection and orgasm. The essential rite of these religions is *castration*, and, in a more civilized way, chastity—or the measureless blind embraces in the temples of India and Egypt, of Phoenicia and Syria, which correspond, in an opposite sense, to castration and chastity.

Circumcision may also be considered, from this point of view, as an equivalent of castration—and one should not be astonished at this additional meaning: each of these ritual acts may really have an infinite number of coexisting meanings, for infinite, also, are the terrors and the gods.

In order to know that these ambiguous deities, which are both day and night, summer and winter, sun and moon, man and woman, compel us to the sacrifice of abstinence and castration—each of us need only look inside himself. Blushing cheeks are evidence enough, without resorting to the thousands of observations made by psychiatrists and biologists, to the thousands of novels and tragedies which tell with infinite variety of moods the same romance of sacred terror and religious sacrifice. The impotence peculiar to youth is a religious defense against a premature communion, which would mean the loss of self. If a person has not yet acquired a distinct shape, how could he possibly unite with another one without melting away, or even perceive the other one's existence? Love and liberty are born together.

All things considered, sacred love is an impossibility: it leads to death even before the start. Such love, made religion, prevents its own fulfillment and thus procures salvation from that death. A voiceless abyss where all seeds are mingled, a shoreless sea which no eye may behold, a crossing from which no living soul ever returns—this is sacred love: deep black waters.

Nevertheless, in these waters, somebody is preening himself and smiling at himself, somebody who is everybody: Narcissus. Man is not yet adult; he is not free enough to recognize the *other*; but the need of love is born already, a need which makes one's own self appear as the other, and which turns inward the groping of desire. Inside, where there is nothing but waters and depth, Narcissus thinks to find another self, responding to his smile, another self which may be loved as an equal, and not dreaded like a woman or a god. But this other one is merely an image, an aerial fantasy—and this embrace too, is mortal.

Narcissus has always existed, even before the Greeks made him into a graceful myth: he is eternal. But the time which truly fits him best is that in which a vital yearning for liberty and love is thwarted or not yet fully grown: therefore, the seventeenth century, the *seicento* lifts the sign of Narcissus upon its banners in Caravaggio's style, and reacts to the Counter-Reformation by shrinking into its own self, by retiring into its innermost depth, mirrored in the sensuous curves of the baroque. This was a time like our own, of prisons and youthful solitude:

> From my solitudes I come,
> To my solitudes I go,

For, to stay with my own self,
My thoughts are company enough.[7]

Not in this solitude, still anarchical, but in another and demo-
cratic one, in the midst of the numberless crowd, stands the man
who is too grown up, who is entirely segregated, limited and individual, entirely out of touch with the indefinite common, deprived
of sacred powers and sacred terrors, and living without freedom
and without gods. Others are present, of course, but inaccessible,
because there no longer exists the tie that could unite them in
mutual comprehension. Human relations are wholly external, and
very easy, because they are non-existent. Modesty, restraint, truth-
fulness, chastity, impotence make no sense any more, and there
are no more interdictions, or servitude, except the bonds of interest
and usage. Even reality is gone; profane love is no love, and it does
not lead to a death only because it proceeds from a death. Miser-
able are the triumphs of the individual:

Old ones also are his pleasure
For the boast of a full measure[8]

until the terror of his own barrenness drives him again into idolatry.
One single and definite woman becomes the goddess of a private
cult; and rarely indeed does she attain, by grace of poetry, the level
of the divine. Servitude of love requires its own rites and mutilations, its own hatreds and wars: to nurture his idol, the worshipper
must give his life away, while wounding and despising the deity

---

7. A mis soledades voy de mis soledades vengo
   de mis soledades vengo
   porque para andar conmigo
   me bastan mis pensamientos.
   ("A mis soledades voy," Lope de Vega [1562–1635])
8. Delle vecchie fa conquista
   pel piacer di porle in lista
   (From the libretto of Mozart's *Don Giovanni* by Lorenzo Da Ponte)

itself. The rite that fits this religion of love is *sadism*: without the double sacrifice of self and of the idol beloved, worship vanishes and love is possible no more. Hence, the offences and injuries, the deceits and lies and blows, the mortifications and murders. A definite person is made sacred, because of her very definiteness and limitation: the entire world, therefore, must shrink to these limits, must lose its freedom and universality, and become this single object of love. In this confined horizon and idolatrous wretchedness, in the sweetness of these chains, the narrower the space in the accepted prison, the more one feels inclined to totally adore. In such a drying up and shriveling of the soul every self-inflicted mutilation seems holy, every humiliation and abasement acceptable in order to reach a complete religious fixation. Circe, the divine magician, goes on and on eternally taking from her adorers their likeness of men and turning them into beasts, into dogs and swine; and they, barking and grunting, express their joy and delight.

As the worshiper offers to his deity the sacrifice of his own human nature, so the idol itself must also be sacrificed: and it is a true idol only if downtrodden, offended, restricted, diminished. Not only does the beloved forsake her quality as a person, but even her appearance and the integrity of her shape—shrinking to a material part, to a leg, to a head of hair, to a breast, to a gown, to a mere object. And the love focused upon this object turns into a cruel revenge for all that has been lost. Even further than that: the idol-object ceases to have any connection with the person beloved, and becomes a fetishistic symbol, one of the thousands which psychoanalysts have so carefully classified. The more limited and precise and corporeal this symbolic object, the greater its divine potency: a glove, a picture, an excrement become irresistible, irreplaceable, amorous deities, absolute tyrants.

Thus, in the private and tender and daily field of love, we are confronted with the same vicissitudes as in the field of the relationship between man and the state. Outside the freedom of a person completed, able therefore to conceive the other, to identify itself with the other in a common human nature, there is nothing but a sacred death in primeval indistinction, or a death profane in barren distinctness. Between the two impossible opposites of sacred love and love profane, any attempt at religious salvation is nothing but castration or sadism, puritanism or libertinage, extremes born of one single process. Between these two coincident extremes forever oscillate religious lovers. It is the old problem of spirit and body, which have contended since the very inception of time. The historical transition between the reign of the *Roi Soleil* and the Regency, or between the Victorian era and Lawrence's priapic revolution, is taking place continually and without hope of salvation in every man, incapable of freedom, who has made of his affections an idol, and offered sacrifices and offered up his self.

Love is not only the elementary human relationship, the first discovery of the world, the touchstone of liberty, it is also procreation, family, and therefore society and state. The point of interest here is not how love may exist, but how it may serve the greater deities of the fathers, of the clan, the tribe, the state. And certainly it is love, in its free and individual nature, which must be sacrificed to these gods. When the father is god, there is no room for love: woman is a slave, not an equal. The gravest offence is adultery, solely because it means a betrayal of God (jealousy is a divine sentiment, an impious deed, a siding with the enemy, with a stranger, with another god). Therefore, the adulterous woman is sacred, deserving of death, untouchable. Only a god son, who does not know of foreign deities, can look upon her with pity, and send her home alive. The father chooses brides for his sons, and sells his daughters as mere commodities. Jacob finds in his bed a woman he does not want, and pays with seven years of servitude for the wife of his choice, thus rendering homage to the divine authority of his father Laban: and only as a girl in love could Laban's daughter, portending a more exalted God, steal for love's sake the deities of the father, humble herself in hiding them, and sit upon them, in the camel's saddle.[9]

For the tribe, ancient or modern, that worships not a familiar but a collective god, women are common property: adultery and

---

[9.] Genesis 19.18–35, 31.1–42.

sacrilege is only that which is committed outside the tribe, there where another sacred animal holds its sway. In the tribe too, but even more so in the paternal state, women have no gods of their own, and are ruled solely by the deities of their menfolk. Women may therefore be ravished by the foe, and even if born at home, they always remain strangers, because they take part in the rites only as victims. Love is impossible when it is thus turned into servitude. What counts is not the certitude of love, but that of matrimony, of children, of the family. Woman is sacrificed to the father-god. The mythical founders of cities have no human father; they are the sons of gods, of sacred virgins, of animals. They never could have separated from a true father to establish another patrician city-state: therefore their birth must be mysterious. So that Jesus might speak of love, he had to be a son without a father—and his voice truly opened locked doors. But the divine fathers and the divine States live eternally, and jealously claim, throughout eternity, the slavery of woman and the sacrifice of love.

Nudo (**Nude**, 1942)

As long as there is one single slave, everybody shares his servitude.

4 / Slavery

Admission into Oriental and Grecian mysteries was gained through the initiation of sacrifice. Fasting, abstinence, purification, chastity, mutilations, macerations, renouncement of love or modesty were the indispensable preliminaries, and perhaps the mystery which the believer could then behold was nothing but a sacred pageant, where the same sacrifices were performed by the gods; a symbolic performance, revealing the symbol, but not the symbol's meaning, which remained, even to the initiated, mysterious in its multiplicity, ambiguous and infinite, like terror and like the gods themselves. All the interpretations, from the grossest to the most sublime, which are rediscovered with such learned ingenuity to explain these ancient rites, may be quite true, but none of them is satisfactory: because, in truth, the rite resolved itself into the symbol and did not require explanation. The mortal vagueness, from which escape was sought, resided not in reason, but in feeling—and therefore the symbolic liberation had to be perceived through feeling, not through reason. A voluntary servitude gives birth to the idols; it is by itself an initiation; it breaks away from the worlds both of indeterminate and of personal life, and thus creates another world, where life is ritual, a world most truly powerful when evident in its appearance and mysterious in its meaning.

The life of every single individual, and the entire history of mankind, taken as a religious history and life, may be considered as one great mystery, in which every man and every historical period gain admission and initiation at every moment, in each fraction of time. It is a mystery, obscure to reason, but crystal clear to religious feeling, which seeks only a limited, perceptible, evident certitude. And this mystery, this history, is one eternal sacrifice, which alone enables the weirdness of myth to change into the mysterious certainty of ritual. The horrid darkness of night swarms, for the child, with monsters which still seem frightful only because they fail to take a definite shape: but imagining monsters is already an attempt at religious liberation. The discovery of women—an unutterable incertitude—turns into tyranny, fetishism, sadism; the darkness of family communion turns into patriarchy. Even man's relation to his own creative powers is made certain and definite through idolatry: creation becomes *work*, a malediction from heaven. Language itself loses its vital and poetical meaning, and tends to become symbolical, evocative and magical, confining itself to clear formulations, fully of practical power and devoid of meaning:

> . . . Speak lower, Mnasylus: the gods
>   are everywhere,
> Hecate's eye divine is gleaming from
>   the dark.[1]

says the Parnassian poet. But how can we hide, when every action of ours, every word, is a deity?

Eternal renouncement, ceaselessly renewed, nurtures the idol and is itself an idol, connecting the image of the past with that of the future by a tie which seems historical and is in fact religious. In this way, individual life finds continuity through a continuous self-denial, and man makes of his own self a stranger and a victim.

That which goes for the individual applies also to society and to the state. The state-idol can exist only through a process of social

---

1. Parle bas, les dieux sont partout, ô Mnasyle,
    Hécate nous regarde avec son oeil divin.
    ("Le Chevrier," from José-Maria de Hérédia [1842–1905], *Les trophées*)

alienation and sacrifice: only through *slavery*. Slavery and divineness of the state are exactly the same: the divine nature of the state is slavery, and slavery could not exist without the state's divinity, for deity and victim coincide.

The civilizations of antiquity, where the state rests upon religion, are based upon slavery, derive their origin from slavery, and would not be conceivable without it: in vain do moralists and philosophers deplore the fact of slavery as a disgrace, as a blemish upon the face of an otherwise heavenly star. True, these civilizations are not exclusively religious; but their state organization is founded on a religious world. Slavery is therefore an absolutely inseparable and essential element of their structure. Hence, all the movements of servile rebellion are doomed to failure: in no mythology were gods ever overthrown and struck down by victims—only by fearless, innocent or wise men. Giants may scale Olympus and dark angels storm the skies: but they are confined within the world which they have accepted, which is theirs, without which they would not exist—and the gods can smile at their revolt. Spartacus naturally falls—because his rebellion is absurd as long as he clings to a slave's banner and recognizes implicitly both slavery and the divinity of the state. This is the necessary fate of all movements of revolt in which the victim objects to the knife, but not to the altar; the fate of every attempt (however humanely legitimate) which starts as a demand for liberation, that is, for abstract justice, and not for liberty itself. For the state-idol, the institution of slavery is vital law, and therefore concrete justice. The revolt of the slaves may at most lead to a reversal of functions; it may, as in some imaginary drawing by Goya, turn the goat into the sacrificer.[2] This is, as we shall see, the true weakness of those proletarian movements which not without reason have fondly called themselves by the ill-omened name of Spartacism; and, generally, the weakness of all those movements, be they of ever so radical an appearance, which do not step beyond the religious limits of the civilization they try to supersede.

---

2. Levi is referring here to Goya's *Goat* or *Witches Sabbath* (1820–1823), now in the Prado Museum of Madrid.

For the state to be a god, man in his entirety, man the essence of state, must become enslaved; and all men are enslaved, from the king to the meanest pariah. To be precise, as long as there is one single slave, everybody shares his servitude. However, sacrifice being a symbol, universal servitude must be symbolized by somebody in particular, somebody whose specific function is, for all men's sake, to take this servitude upon himself, to display it ostensibly, to become for all men a stranger to the state, and for all men the victim. In an organic state, the institution of slavery is a *necessary* organ, the one which allows the other organs to enjoy some relative freedom. Not only the patricians and plebeians, but also the slaves, first of all the slaves, should have been mentioned in the famous fable by Menenius Agrippa[3] about the irreplaceable members of the social body—and he did not mention them perhaps because they are sacred and therefore unmentionable; or maybe the metaphor was not a happy one, because they are the parts of a divine, not of a human body.

Who therefore, as a consecrated victim, shall bear upon his shoulders the divinity of the state? Who shall support the state without being a part of it? Evidently the strangers: those who are of alien origin as well as those who become alien by exercising a function considered as fitting the aliens: conversely, the activity of strangers shall appear as a servile occupation. Foreign men and foreign things, more than all the others, seem to be a divine quality; by their very nature, by the very fact of their strangeness and hostility, they are sacred things, to be sacrificed.

In warlike states, whose gods are gods of battle, the slaves become first of all the prisoners. Slaves fit for sacrifice, to be slaughtered on the altars, or to be kept alive, in order to perform those functions that are strange to the military state: the general functions of manual and mechanical work, which for the warrior are

---

3. Livy tells how Menenius Agrippa's fable—about how each part of the body is necessary for the proper functioning of the whole, with the stomach representing the patrician class and the various limbs standing for the plebeians—was decisive in easing tensions in the "Struggle of the Orders" in early Rome.

disgraceful, and therefore sacred; and also the more peculiarly disgraceful functions of the so-called infamous occupations, sometimes including commerce, and even medicine and philosophy. These were, approximately, the functions of the slaves in Rome. Because of their existence, the plebe was never comparable to the modern proletariat or a lower class; it was a kind of middle class, which, although it had to struggle for centuries before gaining full rights and transforming patrician law into a citizens' law, was never entirely in bondage. The existence of slavery allowed for relative plebeian liberty and the freedom of civil struggles. It also allowed the union between the warrior gods of the fathers and the rustic gods of the most ancient Italians; the fusion (which has never been complete) of two quite different trends; the original grafting of a military, state-worshiping, religious, juridical civilization upon a rustic civilization which was anarchical, irreligious and poetical. Here we may find the reason why Roman expansionism was a necessity: the freedom of Rome's citizens required an ever growing servitude. The fertile civil struggles could develop only with the help of foreign wars: so that Rome might be free, the entire world had to fall into slavery.

Where slaves cannot be captured in war, or bought for money, in states which are self-contained, weak or pacific, the citizens themselves must be enslaved, through a process of expulsion and differentiation. Castes, closed guilds and hierarchy are born. In Egypt, a country of cities and sedentary agriculture, dependent upon the river and the seasons, the lowest caste was considered as the most foreign: the nomads, the swineherds and shepherds. In the Oriental fables, sorceresses turn the prince into a swineherd, the last degree of human slavery. The wandering Hebrews were slaves, both as strangers and as herdsmen.

The castes of India result from the crystallizing of an extremely complex history; they are bred by a religiosity which is more social than political. The Indian state is nothing but an idol of the very hierarchy of bondage. In the overflowing sacred and corresponding religiousness, every action, every relation, every contact becomes impossible and forbidden. Closed worlds living in mutual ignorance coexist in infinite numbers, like the infinity of the gods. Each has its own interdictions, each is shameful and untouchable for the others. Here the religion of human relationship, born of the incumbent fear of confusion, has destroyed the state, turning it into a dead impossibility.

The history of the Hebrews, considered as a sacred history, or rather, as a mythology (and we are not dealing here with their religious and profane history, which is that of a small Oriental people incessantly struggling between transcendency and idolatry), negates every idol that is an enemy of the Lord. The entire people had been slaves in Egypt and were to be slaves in Babylon, and again in times to come: voluntary servitude, for they had sacrificed to the idols. But after they gain faith in the transcendent God, which is not a god of human relations, that is—after they renounce every state-idolatry, the people are no longer the slaves of men. They shall be only the servants of God, "for unto me the children of Israel are servants;[4] they are my servants who I brought forth out of the land of Egypt," (that is—of idolatry) "and they shall not be sold as bondsmen."[5] They have no state, they do not live tied to the earth, "for the land is mine, for ye are strangers and sojourners with me."[6] Thus, there cannot be slavery upon earth: but the people, eternally foreign to the earth, are chosen to be the servants and victims of divine transcendency.

After the transformation of the Roman republic—a people's republic and city-state—into an Empire embracing all the nations of the known world, the time was ripe for Christian preaching, which extended the gift of election to all men and tried to sever them, in matters of faith, from the earthly fathers and from every idol of state and society. Moreover, the classical form of Roman slavery, whose institutions were characteristic of a military state, at once aristocratic and popular, was bound to fall into decay after the consolidation of the monarchy. Slavery was becoming softer,

---

4. Leviticus 25.55.
5. Leviticus 25.42.
6. Leviticus 25.23.

its limits were now easy to cross; the right of citizenship, formerly almost unobtainable, because it entailed participation in the divinity of the state, could now be acquired with more ease; and this is only logical, because citizenship, that is the divinity of the city, as well as slavery in its traditional form, which provides victims for the paternal deities and later for the city-gods, was gradually losing its value and significance. As long as family gods were in power, gods of patrician nobility, gods of city and society, these particular deities required particular victims, and slavery therefore embraced everything which was strange to the clan's nobility and the city's tradition. Under the deified monarch, the state being gathered in *one*, the ancient slavery, manifold and particular, loses its meaning. Under the king, everybody is a servant: the unity of the idol requires the totality of the victims. This explains how slavery, which had been within precise limits a well-defined institution of the state, becomes under the Empire a fundamental principle permeating the entire state—so that the loosening of the former bonds of slavery entails the loss of every personal and civic freedom. The state becomes orientalized; society is turning into a mass without shape or limits. The idolatrous reverence for the state is growing stronger, and every single man, unable to be a member of the body politic, an active and effective bearer of the entire polity, turns to the only possible participation, to the last means by which to avoid the loss of every human relationship, and becomes a worshiper, a servant and victim of the state. Total servitude has to be organized; the castes originate, in which the common ritual of devotion to the state is allowed to combine with a thousand other particular rites of social devotion. Thus, upon the ruins of former liberty and former slavery, the guilds come to life; and they are born with the hallmark of trade—which alone differentiates the members of a shapeless mass—and with the sign of the sepulchre, with the sign of the religion of the dead, which alone attempts salvation from the eternal dissolving indistinctness.

The return of barbarism has really nothing in common with primitive barbarism, for there always endures in it a feeling for the singleness of the state, despite the infinite multiplicity of states; and thus there coexist with the numberless dragons and lions, horses and monsters of barbarism, the eagles of empire, these solitary oceanic birds; with the numberless feudal and particular servitudes, the general and terrestrial bondage to the Holy Empire; and the celestial bondage to the only god is not forgotten, despite the existence of innumerable minor deities, of countless relics, all of them holy. Thus, while men still believe in one God, wars are waged to deprive the foe of the gods they adore, of their saintly relics, of their idols, and therefore of their particular freedoms. Thus, slavery is simultaneously a general principle, underlying the common hierarchic life, and particular institution, connected with each single god. In other words, all men are servants, in a greater or lesser measure, to the only king: but, as the various deities have returned to the soil, to the woods of the hunter, deep down to the ground, the servants of servants have become the serfs of the soil. The tilling of fields, the most human of toils, is strange to an earth which is divine in its savage nature, in its naked powers, and which is subdivided not according to the varying cultures and crops, but solely according to limits set by the violent rule of some heraldic beast. Therefore, the labor of fields is the labor of serfs, victims of an earth which has again become sacred. And not only work in the fields, but work in general is foreign to these gods of violence and honor—work which in times religious and sacred cannot but remind us of a time more human and anticipate future days of freedom. Particularly commerce is strange to these gods, which are tied to the earth, to a piece of earth the size of whatever their falcon-eyes may be able to encompass, or of whatever may extend under the walls of the castle. What men are these, obstinate against the ties, attempting to infuse the lifeblood of economy into a crystallized world, and creating contacts between secluded lands, without roads, each with its own local god, lordly self-sufficient? Their activity is foreign to the new religious civilization; it is therefore a sacred and contemptible activity, privileged and subject to arbitrary taxation. In the feudal civilization there is no place but that of a victim for the merchant— and commerce, not without reason, is an achievement of the Jews, of this people without idols, perforce strangers to escutcheons, to emblems and to gods. It was a necessity that such a foreign people should exist, to carry on an activity which, however necessary, was incompatible with the deities of fountains and lakes, of forests and castles: it was necessary that custom and law should render this people more and more explicitly foreign, that they should segregate its members in the most radical manner and oppose every attempt at fusion, that they should exclude them from humanity so that their necessary function would not offend those sedentary gods, those gods of strongholds whose task it was to firmly establish the nests and boundaries, the limits and interdictions of a world which had grown to be limitless, boundless and open. Serfs bound to the furrow, like crawling animals, *animaux rampants*, as they appeared to La Bruyère;[7] or merchants of a people made strangers to men, (or belonging to the republics of seafarers, for the fluid gods of the sea are quite unlike the gods of forests and hills): necessary mutilations, inevitable sacrifices, giving life to the thousand new gods of feudal hierarchy, which were to save mankind from the terror of a new sacred confusion.

A confusion of rights and peoples, of races and nations and languages and gods; a universal return to the sacred silence of shapelessness, such is the meaning of the Roman Empire in the period usually described as that of its decline and fall. The frontiers extended to the limits of the world, the many languages merged in one, all the peoples mixed together, all the powers concentrated in a single point, and the fullness of servitude weighing upon all—the world of men was returning to its first state of a chaotic mass, sacred, ineffable, undifferentiated. Ancient slavery had lost its meaning, for it was an articulate slavery, a class slavery, indispensable for the freedom of other classes. Similarly, all the gods of antiquity were fading away, merging their respective attributes and rituals, since the particular fears and the particular needs of liberation from which they were born were dissolving into the unity of a new terror. This sacred reflowering engulfed the ancient traditions of countries

---

7. Jean La Bruyère (1645–1696) was a French essayist whose *Caractères* of 1688 gained him admission to Académie Française in 1693.

grown old as well as the fresh impulses of barbarian newcomers. Idle were the attempts at restoring the deities of old—classical polytheism was reaching its end amid the anguishing indistinctness of a limitless world, of a nameless and speechless mass, of a vague mysterious forest. Feudal religion, by creating a new slavery and a new privilege, was again dividing the forest according to certain boundaries and giving the world an iron frame to prevent its disintegration; feudalism was driving out a part of man so that life might continue, and circumcising itself in order to gain consecration. The symbols of the countless new gods, the rites of the numberless new victims were creating new religious languages, and thus giving mankind a new *practical* means of expression. Until the day of liberty's return (return as a fundamental and visible element of civil life, for naturally, neither in man nor in mankind had liberty ever entirely disappeared): a day when freedom would create new languages, a new ideal perspective, a new culture and a new poetry.

Donne furenti (Furious women, 1934)

We have all of us struggled until dawn with the Angel, and the Angel did not tell us his name . . . but this struggle has left its mark upon each of our works . . . the reflection of a religious vision.

5 / The Muses

With the dissolving of the Roman world into an imperial society essentially inorganic, the Latin language also dies and disappears. That a language, the one language of an entire world, spoken by every people under every sky, should by and by become incomprehensible and empty, and grow into a thousand shapes of baby talk, may seem a miracle, but not a greater one than each man's daily aging and continuous rebirth.

The world of the Empire, in its universal servitude, in its colossal uniformity, deprived human relations of all their freedom, and despoiled them of every particular religion: there was no place any more for the person, but only for a single shapeless mass, and the altars stood empty, stripped of the old gods. It was vain, then as always, to turn back: the philosophers and politicians who sought for the lost freedom in a society and in a cult which were already dead, could place it only in the abstract individual, in his virtue and conscience; and these philosophers were turning into noble statues of salt, stoically barren. Their Latin therefore became a secret language, understood by the initiated only.

But the shapeless mass, the initial human chaos, is speechless. Its unity is pure inexpressible power. Every word is implicit therein, all languages merged in confusion—but nothing can be uttered: a single spoken word would open the dark womb. Therefore the ancient Latin tongue withdraws from the lips as well as the thoughts, and the open clarity of expression gives way ever more to a human silence, full of every terror and every possibility.

Not from the abstract profoundness of the individual conscience, nor from bright stoical virtue are born the new gods, but from another depth: from the depth of the earth, and from the glitter of arms. Latin remained the sacred language of a divinity imperial and dead. New gods were shaping new religious languages, but at the same time, as the mass was differentiating, and freedom dimly dawning again, new poetical languages were also coming to life.

There exists a religious language, which at first may be a mute language, consisting of signs, of attitudes; in a family religion it is made up of names and possessions, in a feudal religion, of fiefs, coats of arms, badges, banners, weapons, usages, impositions, manumissions, declarations, and so forth. There is also a religious language which is spoken and figurative, made up of sacred images and of prayers. And finally, the entire language, inasmuch as it has a symbolic and not an expressive value, is a religious language; every word contains in itself a god, and, eternally true to itself, represents the god and turns it into an object. Religion is the individuating limitation of that which has no shape, the symbolical fixation of the indeterminate. Religion's expression always refers to something that is beyond it, to a transcendent deity or to a deified object which always remains outside the symbol. Religious language is therefore inexpressive by its very nature. A prayer should not make any sense; a prayer is more efficacious when pronounced in a dead language or in a language which is not understood: however, like every symbol, a prayer must be precise, well defined, and capable of infinite repetition. Its aim is not the creation of thought, but of certainty. Such is the entire language of heraldry: insignia and banners do not represent the fief or the nation, but they are the sign of the fief's and nation's certainty and divineness.

Religious language has no value in itself, but only in relation with the object symbolized: therefore this language must be together inexpressive and perfectly clear. Playing cards are perfect religious images: quite rightly, therefore, are they used for drawing lots and divining the future.

Religious language originates from a need of fixation and certitude. The religious images or words, in their limitation, take the place of a frightful reality—and they must be capable of identical repetition, so as to free us, through their immutability, from that terrible changefulness which they come to replace. The crest makes the earl, the flag makes the nation, the cognomen makes the family, the uniform makes the army, the prayers make the god. They make him a certainty, a practical reality—not an image—a living reality which cannot be repeated.

Religious expression is therefore the contrary of poetical expression. The former is a symbolic limitation of the universal, the latter—the concrete expression thereof; the one is the manifested certainty of a divine, liberating servitude, the other is the voice itself of human liberty; on the one hand—fixed ritual, on the other—mythology. Strictly speaking, one cannot ascertain a "before" and an "after," neither individually nor historically, between these two contradictory expressions—but only a complementary alternation. The child is born mute, and cannot speak as long as it remains an unlimited being, uncertain and chaotic: its cries are vague and impersonal like the rustling of leaves. But although its expressions are poetical or religious, according to its development as a person or its adherence to custom, and although, beneath the prevailing ritual (for the child's world is essentially religious) the personal myths, born of true facts or of the creative imagination, make their appearance—nevertheless, the child's first language consists in great part of magic formulas, endowed with great evocative and practical efficiency. The true live speech develops later on, with the maturing of the person, with the discovery of the world, which cannot be summoned up at the sound of a prayer, but which unfolds and takes shape through the warmth of love.

Art may be considered as a *mythology* (if by the word "myth" we mean the expression of a particular spiritual world), inasmuch as art should be referred to that element of feeling which conditions it, and which in it is merged and exhausted. Art is a totality, for both the element of indeterminateness and that of particularity originate there, and the abyss takes shape without losing depth, and passion expresses itself without howling, and man appears entire, unfettered, sufficient unto himself. Strictly speaking, there is no religious art: to say there is would be a contradiction in terms. Art resolves within itself, without residue, the entire moral and religious world, as well as the vague areas of sentiment and feeling. And, whenever religion is told in terms of poetical myth, it is mere poetry, and no longer religion. The Bible itself, as the mythology of the Hebrew people, is nothing but a work of art; it becomes a moral and theological code only when these myths are being severed from their particular and historical expression, from their peculiar and unique value that is, when they are no longer interpreted as myths, but as symbols of a truth which lies outside them, and which, being eternally the same, renders them fit for eternal repetition. The live characters of Tolstoy are myths of absolute happiness, of total youthful freedom: the others, who have no artistic reality, remain the symbols of a world of moral velleities. D. H. Lawrence's most convincing figures are myths of an eternal puritan struggle between body and soul—but they live, through their hopeless ventures and provisory solutions, in a manner which is unique; the other figures, artistically unsuccessful, give us the religious symbols of this struggle: a white bird, and a wooden turgidity. In other words, art creates myths even when its abstract content is religious; and religion believes in symbols, even when the world from which it arises is a world of freedom. Religious expression is a need of certainty—certainty not only of that which has no shape, but even of that which has form and life. Every word becomes religious when one thinks of it as possessing a value and a meaning *in itself*, as capable of remaining significant by itself—that is, as something which symbolizes another reality, permanent and transcendent, to which it is the magical key. Every rhythm, every rhyme turns into things religious whenever, instead of arising together with the verse, they are left to remain like a scaffolding, like an external sign of poetry. All language is inexpressively religious inasmuch as it serves to endow us through its symbols with a sure and practical means of contact, inasmuch as it serves to represent schematically our needs and actions, and, at the sacrifice of creativity, to give us the certitude of an external relationship, the feeling of a space and time extraneous to thought, and immutable. Finally, art is religious in its entirety when the living myths thereof become for the artist mere symbols of their own selves, as happens in every period marked by "the religion of Art," as well as in the life of every single artist. There follows an external artistic continuity, which is not so much a sign of the permanence of a certain personal world, as indeed an act of faith in certain forms grown symbolic and divine: an act by which one renounces the peril of creative freedom, and obtains—through sacrifice—a certainty. Most of an artist's changes, in style or period, are religious crises arising in some private artistic religion of his own: he needs to get rid of the old and dead symbols in order to create new myths and escape fixation.

Popular art is eminently religious, in all its forms—figurative, musical, architectural, poetical, as well as those that merge with habit, dress and custom, and with the thousand rites which accompany life. Popular art is simply the fixation and perpetuation of moods and means originally expressive, which have lost their former peculiar significance and turned into stereotyped and merely symbolic expressions. Not only the objects of popular devotion, such as fetishes, the statuettes of family-gods, the images endowed with miraculous powers, the figures of saints and Madonnas, the formulas of exorcism and magic, but even artistic objects with no perceivable religious content, such as the dolls, the obscene scribblings on walls, the songs and ditties of love, the traditional shapes given to loaves of bread and to other familiar things, the decorative sculptures of fountains, houses, utensils and tools, the ceremonials of cooking and eating, etc.—are nothing but symbols, where the only value resides in the certainty of the thing or idea represented, while the way of representing it is fixed, and therefore non-expressive and solely religious. It is precisely the sameness of the representation which confers to the latter its value and authority: it is the process of prayer and sacrifice. The fixity of style is the characteristic of popular art—as well as of children's art, if we are to believe Alain, who says that children live in a world peopled solely by gods.[1]

Religious figuration and artistic expression are antithetical: the latter, a purely human creation, knows no other law than its own, implicit and eternally changeable, even when picturing the objects of religion; the former has the task of *relegating* art to the altar of certitude and duration, of relating and tying it to its own patterns, so that art may continue; of sacrificing it, so that it may become a symbolic tie and relation, and therefore a practical communication between men. The contrast is one of creation and limit. A positive religion is only in part a matter of religiosity; it may even lack any religious content, or it may contain it side by side with the more conspicuous political, historical or sentimental elements: to such a point, that a given religion may represent not so much a religious-ness as an entire civilization—and this necessarily pervades the entire field of art. But the religious vision of the Sistine Chapel, of the *Divine Comedy*, of *Paradise Lost*, or of the *Promessi Sposi*[2] is merely the occasion for a new mythology, which cannot be repeated, and in which the religious motive disappears. Conversely, if religion be the power of limitation, wherein language changes into symbol and the freely created world annuls itself in order to endure—then every artistic activity will appear in the guise of a drama, and its limits will be determined, as by a negative image, by the contours of religion itself. A negative image, reciprocal and reflected. We have all of us struggled until dawn with the Angel, and the Angel did not tell us his name (angels do no express themselves): but this struggle has left its mark upon each of our works; as upon the hip of the Patriarch Jacob: the reflection of a religious vision.

The individual works of art which draw their inspiration from a religious "content" do not constitute in the least a religious art; rather they are an artistic liberation from the gods and the rites they

---

1. Alain, the pseudonym of a French writer (1868–1951) was author of many books; Levi is here referring to his *Dieux*; in English, *The Gods*, trans. Richard Pevear (London: Quartet, 1974).
2. Italy's great national novel, *The Bethrothed* (1825–27), by Alessandro Manzoni (1785–1873).

depict. But in certain periods of history, where the ever present horror of sacredness weighs upon men and compels them to take refuge behind the gods, a diffuse religiosity permeates the least expression, infiltrates the language and shapes it in its own fashion. When the sense of the world is placed outside the world, when every action and every thought are a sacrifice to a deity, language foregoes its autonomous creative value and assumes a symbolic signification. Every part of the language, every single sentence, every word in the sentence becomes a divine symbol: and every symbol, every word has an absolute value, identical with every other, because all of them equally contain and postulate a god. Every symbol must be entire and totally representative: every word becomes valuable, and dwells in isolation. Syntax dissolves: the single elements of a sentence acquire an equal importance, and equally suggestive powers.

Under the compulsion of sacredness, in the urban forest of Rome and the black forest of Germany, the world turns into mass, becomes mute. The Latin tongue disappears: but for a language, to become mute means to undergo mutation. Meanwhile, as a salvation from sacredness, deities arise in infinite numbers and all life dries up in stony religious forms, the new languages themselves are also filled with religiousness, with servitude and interdictions— and even syntax and phonetics are transformed to the core. The one language, Latin, changes into the Romance, or new Latin, languages—according to the particular spirit of the various peoples, who feel, in front of that mortal limitless unity, an obscure need of differentiation.

This linguistic mutation is interpreted by the philologists in terms of phonetics. If we take for instance the formation and transformation of ancient French, the reason for it is sought in the overlong accent with two stresses, which is supposedly characteristic of the Celtic spirit, the Celtic element having merged with the Romanic. But how did it happen, asks Vossler,[3] that this accent, in the first period of medieval French, until approximately the year

---

3. Karl Vossler (1872–1949) was a German linguist and scholar who was deeply influenced by the Italian philosopher-historian Benedetto Croce.

1050, led to progressive displacements, while in the second period it caused displacements which were regressive? Why do diphthongs appear first, and later on—monophthongs? First palatal, and later guttural displacements? First the assimilation, and then the loss of consonants? First the closed syllables, and later the open ones? First the consonantal, and then the vocalic ending of words? First the richness and later the poverty of the phonetic material and of the inflections? The reply, rightly says the German philologist, is to be sought in the style of the language. The diphthong arises when the tonic accents become too frequent, and they are frequent when the structure of speech is *paratactical*.[4] The monophthongs, on the contrary, predominate when the sentence has acquired a tonic balance, and a syntactical construction. And precisely, around the year 1050, both the phonetic and the syntactic mutations take place in medieval French, together with the general change in taste, culture, customs—together with the growth of a new, widespread freedom, and the progressive decay of feudal deities and religious ties.

The primitive expression, that of the world which arose directly from the fall of the Empire and of the Latin language, was an expression, as we have seen, imbued with religiosity. Its syntax, therefore, is paratactical: every word, every image is closed in itself, complete, without ties, and equal in its value to every other one. The images, all equally symbolic, stand side by side, without correlation or opposition: discourse is a *mosaic*. The stress falls upon every word; all of them are on the same plane: there cannot be a *perspective*. Furthermore, as there is no syntactic relationship, every single word must contain in itself the entire concept: inflections are abundant and complicated (dual number, third future tense, etc.).

These considerations about the phonetic expression are also valid with regard to the figurative expressions. Whenever, in a language, the inflections are complicated—in painting, a man viewed

---

4. From the Greek *parataxis*, act of placing side by side. The placing of clauses or phrases one after another without coordinating or subordinating connectives (*Webster's Ninth*).

frontally shall have his face in profile. If stress falls equally on every word all perspective shall be developed on a plane and described without relations; and the relative dimensions of objects are of no importance: a flower or a mountain are both the size of a man, equally symbolic, equally stressed. The greater the poverty of relationship, the richer, the more precious and complicated are the local values and the pictorial matter. When the construction is paratactical, the elements of the pictorial discourse can have, in a painting, only a symmetrical order. In poetry, where the verses are all of one measure, symmetry produces the rhyme, the primitive rhyme which is monotonous. Whereas in words every symbol must be complete in itself, which leads to the formation of diphthongs and consonantal groups of awkward pronunciation, similarly in pictures the gems and golden backgrounds jar side by side with every imaginable tone. The paratactical construction, the symbolic and religious value of expression are thus exalting symmetry and local color, while abolishing tonality and composition. The mosaic, which even materially, technically, is paratactical, becomes the preferred technique.

The art of these Primitives is therefore the art of absolute authority; it has the same characteristics as the Romance languages in their first, early medieval period, the ritual, symbolical, divine period.

The weakening of religiousness through the growth of a sense of humanity, through the liberation of love, through the disappearance of monsters and terrors and the dissolution of hell, creates modern values, modern freedom, modern syntaxes and perspective languages. The *Dolce Stil Novo*, the sweet novel style of early Italian literature, and the painters before Giotto—including Cimabue and Duccio—mark this crisis: Dante and Giotto are at its highest summit, at the powerful whirlwind where intermingle the clashing trends of feudal religion and of liberty. But Masaccio and Boccaccio (these two extraordinary names of disparagement, the one for Thomas, the doubter who touches,[5] the other for the mouth, the most human of our organs, since its function is speech) are already

---

5. John 20.24–29.

entirely engaged *in partibus infidelium*.[6] The ugly is chosen, out of passion for that which is alive; there is no more gold; Latinized prose flows like a stream, involved and syntactical. And if a new religion is born therefrom, it is purely literary religion, a religion of art, mother of academies, of courtly speech, of beautifully inexpressive painting—of all that, alas, which in Italy is usually called the Italian "tradition." But one well understands the enthusiasm of a Paolo Uccello[7] for the discovery of perspective: a liberated world, where everything was relationship, believed it had found the very secret of its liberty. The spiked collar of Paolo Uccello was only a myth—which all too soon became a material symbol in the new worship of perspective, in the architectonic canon of sixteenth-century painting.

The forms of expression in the first period of medieval art were permeated with religious spirit, as we have learned from the language and art of the time. The expressive shapes of the next period, on the contrary, were full of the sense of freedom. These statements should not be understood in a materialistic way—for evidently every work of art, even in the oldest period, was also a work of free creation, the translation into myths of that religious world from which it arose; by the same token, every work of art in the later period was the happy myth of its own free world. In the most primitive period, poetry could originate only from a contrast with the spirit of the time, and was perforce dramatic, and rare as grass in a desert. It was a time of prayer for a humanity that had to gain salvation from the terror of the millennium; and prayer, upon the lips of the cleric and the brush of the painter, came naturally, for the sake of the world's continuance, to make sure that human speech should not be silenced, that it should not cease to be understood, like the tongue of the Giants. This unconscious urge acted like a tremendous drive, giving its sense to every expression. In the following period, the sense was that of poetry, the feeling of a world

---

6. "In the land of unbelievers."
7. Paolo Uccello (1397–1475) was a Florentine painter known for his extraordinary use of perspective.

renewed, which had forgotten the gods and now considered them unnecessary and hostile; a world which was disentangling itself, through the infinitely various liberty of creation, from the shackles and the serfdom of the fathers. These secret currents which give a tonality to an entire epoch, and which are in every man the same, (for all men are driven to avoid the plunge into the sacred, as well as severance from it), are much deeper than that which in the field of art has come to be called "taste." They are that dark necessity which creates differences and frees from dissolution, that necessity through which life endures beyond serfdom and blasphemy and death, until it shines in liberty again; that which makes art painful and contradictory and often partial and miscarrying in time of religion, and which causes the happy art of free times. Therefore is it vain to force upon religion the merit of that which we may call the genius or the feeling or the taste ("the Taste of the Primitives") of a certain period in history. In medieval art, "taste" was at first religious and anti-artistic, and later on poetical and anti-religious. In other times, more recent, and also considered as primitive, the opposite process prevailed: impressionism, the power of freedom, came first, followed later by the returning urge of religiousness. If one can speak of taste, or of genius, or of the general artistic feeling displayed by a certain period, it is precisely because the spirit of the time pervades every organ and form of expression, so that language and art may be taken as *witnesses* of the corresponding civilization, even if they are impeded and almost nullified by it. And, if in certain primitive periods the spirit of the time is a religious spirit, then its true art is an evasion and a drama, and something of a prophecy; for in such periods all other expressions cannot be poetical, but only symbolic and practical. *Ab Jove principium Musae*—neither language nor poetry originates from religion but only the deities of language and poetry, the symbols and rituals of art, the literary genres, the Muses. But a true time of freedom, in its fleeting course, fashions the language and the art of happiness; and sends back into heaven, with the rest of the gods, the sisters Musae—to hide in the divine Father, which men, in all innocence, have by that time forgotten.

Campo di concentramento or *Le donne morte (Il lager presentito)*
(Concentration camp, or Dead women [The camp foreseen], 1942)

But the idols live on forever, in the contemporaneity of times, through thousand shapes forever renewed, and men die in adoration upon their altars, or in the forsaken fields beneath a closed sky.

6 / Blood

For man's indifferent unity, for the woods' fearful darkness, the religious spirit substitutes organized serfdom, and the gods of the garden. For a silence heavy with every possible word and every conceivable poem, a practical means of communication, consisting of symbols and prayers. For the mysterious fusion of man and woman—the reciprocal slavery of love. For the relationship of resemblance, derivation and unavoidable severance between fathers and sons—the Saturnian deity, the sacrifices on the mountains, and civil war.

But sacrifice of freedom, of poetry and love is not enough to confer certainty and truth upon the gods of the state, born of the ambiguousness of human relations. These idols of identity and separation are one with man's soul, for the soul of man is at once identity and separation. This soul, when free, is both individual and universal spirit; but being every time unable (and desperate) to reach the happy point of free identification, the soul would soon revert to chaos or be reduced to dust, unless it turned its own self, where these relations have their place and where the state resides, into a symbolic object of religious adoration. In other words, state-idolatry is an idolatry of the individual soul, unable to achieve the freedom it requires: it is also the need to find an external, enduring certainty—in human relationship a certainty of life, the persistence of heredity through the generations. Soul, life, permanence in time are therefore a necessary idol and a necessary victim. But what is each man's soul and life? What is each man's continuance through time and children?

> "Blood is the life of all flesh; the blood of it is for the life thereof; therefore I said unto the children of Israel: Ye shall eat the blood of no manner of flesh, for the life of all flesh is the blood thereof; whosoever eateth it shall be cut off." ". . . And I have given it to you upon the altar to make an atonement for your souls; for it is the blood that maketh an atonement for the soul."[1]

Blood is sacred, being the very soul; common to all men and every man's own; gushing out entirely from a single wound and eternal through infinite generation. Therefore every god sprung from the need of human relation, every deity of the soul, every symbol of permanence and certitude, holds sacred the blood of man—and blood *alone* can create him. Solemn oaths are sealed with blood; friendship too is a compact of blood. Insults are washed out in blood. Blood engenders mythical dynasties; political outrage, alone, founds tyrannies. Blood raises terror, needless bloodshed is a major sin, a blasphemy. To mention blood is for the Puritans (so attuned to the sacred) the most fearful of curses. Blood is shameful: woman shall be unclean for seven days, and untouchable. Blood is precious: the donors of blood are considered almost heroes for their harmless and easy donation. Blood is a sacrifice which every life requires, it is life itself: woman, this sacred part of man, must shed her blood to know man and to beget man. Blood appears in mysterious dreams. Blood gives birth to idols: while men were born from the dragon's teeth, the blood of men feeds both gods and dragons.

Every divinity which takes the place of the human soul and life requires therefore the sacrifice of human blood. This blood will have to be *shed*, that is poured forth, expelled from the living body, spilled out of the warm, hidden veins, made extraneous to that of which it was the life, and offered on the altar. Only the shed-

---

1. Leviticus 27.14 and 27.11.

ding of human blood makes real the human deities. Without blood, the sacred wedding would not be true: merely a *marriage* instead of holy *matrimony*. The blood-stained sheets are displayed for all to see, and this alone brings forth the matrimonial angels which are to bless the harmony of wedlock. Circumcision in blood introduces the new-born babe to the covenant with that God which it confirms. The Saturnian deities require the bleeding of sons: the fathers must slay the first born in order not to lose the secret attributes of the divine. And the idol-like states are born only in the outpouring of blood, the blood of their own sons and of the enemies, in the mystery of human sacrifice, in the red act of war, begetter of gods.

Personal deities, humanized beasts, double-faced monsters, idols of the individual self, of the family, of the social group, as well as those gods which attend to certain activities or trades or functions of life, or which preside over love, require the sacrifice of human victims, and these deities spring to life the very moment in which the victim dies. The gods themselves must die to procreate: so that the world might be engendered from pre-existent unity, a god—according to the Hindu tale—had to quarter himself in a Bacchic way, to lacerate and slash and cut himself to pieces. And the insects and butterflies, animals perfectly divine, die when they lay their eggs, or are killed while fecundating the female. Men have to die in order to engender the gods: they have to part with their own selves—not merely with their freedom, but even with their blood, the blood they cherish. Blood flows on every altar of every human god, in every clime and every time. Only a greater capacity for symbolism, as well as the aging and decline of faith, permits the sacrifice of animals' blood instead of man's, or the offer of a supposedly equivalent gift, as a reminder of this precious blood. When Bacchus Omestes[2] changed from an Oriental god into a Grecian myth, he allowed the Thebans to offer up a goat instead of the formerly human victim; and despite the contrary advice of the people, who knew the demands of their bull-headed goddess, King

---

2. Bacchus the Devourer.

Agesilaus, according to Plutarch, could sacrifice to the ferocious Diana a deer instead of a maiden. And upon the altars of the same goddess, in memory of a more lethal blood, the youths of Sparta were beaten with rods. The Peruvians used the blood of children, drawn from a little wound on the forehead, to make sweet cakes for the people to eat, in memory of idols, already archaic, which in their days of power were made, materially, of human blood. And in Egypt sacrificial animals were branded by the priest with a mark representing the true victim—a man on his knees, with his hands tied behind his back and a sword about to behead him. But human sacrifice is completely abolished only with the final fall of the human idol: for these two amount to exactly the same thing. When Lycaon is punished by being changed into a wolf while immolating a child to Jupiter Lyceus, when Hercules causes Diomedes, king of Thrace, to be devoured by his own mares, which he used to feed on the flesh of strangers, it means the end of the ambiguous, beast-like idols, the freeing of man from his own monstrous nature, the death of fauns and centaurs. The substitution of a ram for Isaac is a polemic substitution, directed against idolatry, in confirmation of a God entirely transcendent—requiring a victim which has to be not real, but merely symbolic. Hence the abhorrence of blood, the complete interdiction of shedding blood or of eating it with meat, actions which in themselves are idolatrous: for blood creates the idols and is itself an idol. The animal's blood is not allowed to remain in the meat, or to be shed outside the Tabernacle: and if anyone be guilty of killing an animal elsewhere, "blood shall be imputed unto that man: he hath shed blood, and that man shall be cut off from among his people."[3] Blood is idol and demon, and generates idols and demons.

As long as the deity and the idol coincide, sacrifice must remain absolutely material: and where the idol is human, the victims must be human too, for every god must die in order to gain life. Substitution of the victim takes place only when the god,

---

3. Leviticus 27.4.

ceasing to be an idol, leaves the earth and the body and makes his ascent to heaven and the conscience; for how is it possible to kill a hidden god, a god no one may see nor call by name? Strictly speaking, sacrifice should be abolished altogether, even in its symbolic form: but, although God is transcendent, he leaves behind some Law, some symbol of the divineness of moral conscience, as an idol of enduring certitude—and to this Law, to this Covenant are due the symbolic sacrifices. Identification of man and God cannot arise without divine and human blood, without the blood of Christ. But this blood too, outside the person of Christ, is still for men a mere symbol, a wine, a religion, and that which ought to be the truest liberty remains even now a practical and ritual liberation.

The Gods must die and bleed in order to exist.

"For where a testament is, there must of necessity be the death of the testator. . . . Wherefore neither the first testament was dedicated without blood. . . . For when every commandment had been spoken by Moses unto all the people according to the law, he took the blood of calves and of goats . . . and sprinkled both the book and all the people, saying: This is the blood of the covenant which God hath enjoined unto you."[4]

"It was necessary therefore that the copies of the things in the heavens should be cleansed with these" (with the animals' blood); "but the heavenly things themselves with better sacrifices than these. For Christ entered not into a holy place made with hands, which is a figure of the true; but into heaven itself."[5]

"Neither by the blood of goats and calves, but by his own blood, he entered once into the holy place, having obtained eternal redemption."[6]

Once says Paul, and forever: the sacrifice of God should be the last of human sacrifices. But the idols live on forever, in the contemporaneity of times, through thousand shapes forever renewed,

---

4. Hebrews 9.16–20.
5. Hebrews 9.23–24.
6. Hebrews 9.12.

and men die in adoration upon their altars, or in the forsaken fields beneath a closed sky.

If Christ himself is born of blood, if every man hopes to become immortal, to become a god by way of his own true death, how can the divinity of the state originate without killings, slaughters and war? Banners are sacred only when stained with the blood of citizens, and the greatest national monument is the tomb of an unknown soldier.

For the state-divinity, war is a perfect sacrifice, the victims offered up being the enemies, those who are strangers to the god; and also the god himself, his representatives, the members of the state, the warriors. Those among the enemy who have not been killed in battle rightly become slaves—and the slaves are sacrificed on the altars, or spared for servile tasks: victims, always, of the same idol. Conversion is useless, often impossible, seldom offered; proselytes are not required, but strangers to the particular god and to mankind itself, strangers fit to be immolated. Only when a more universal deity stands beside or above the god of the state, is it possible to conciliate opposed interests and differing cults, so that the prisoners are speedily and collectively baptized, as the Spaniards did to the Mexicans, whom they initiated to the kingdom of heaven, before exterminating them *ad majorem Dei gloriam*, to the glory of that other god, who reigned in Madrid over his earthly kingdom. However, baptized or not, converted or not, the spoils of war are always *opimae*, sacred to the goddess of state, host to be sacrificed.

Every war is a duel of gods, a judgment of God, in the double sense of judgment: for God is both the judge and the judged. Only the victorious god is judged to be existing and true: victory is the proof of his birth and of his power, and of his sacred legitimacy. Slaughtering prisoners and defeated enemies is not only legitimate, but imperative in religious war—and it is foolish and pointless to be shocked by the bombing of open cities and the death of infants, in battles fought for the sake of an idol. These prisoners and vanquished, these women and children are not protected by gods, they have no idols of power and life; and thus they do not belong to the world of rites, they are aliens, vanquished people, doomed to be bound in chains, turned into slaves and immolated as victims: *victi* and *victimae*.

Wars follow and mirror the nature of the god for whom they are waged and with whom they merge. The manifold deities of heroic times live in continuous individual contests; feudal deities war on all frontiers, on every level, in every estate. Divinities belonging to large, national and imperial states, wage more extensive wars, national and world-wide. But always the idolatric sense of the state requires war, ceaseless and total, a war which is one with the state and the state's existence, inseparable from the life of the god.

Only the state of liberty is a state of peace: where there is true peace, there is true freedom, for idols cannot live without war; but men live only in peace. It is peace, because the human person, in its particularity, forms the entire state, and the state in its particularity, is all person, all mankind. Nothing is extraneous to the state—to the state of liberty—in the true sense of this maxim (which is generally used in reverse): it means that nothing human is alien to man, when man has not assigned limits unto himself, when his freedom allows him to reach at the same time personal individuation and limitless universality. But everything is foreign to the state, when the state is an idol, a limit, and therefore in itself a thing providentially foreign. Everything must become extraneous to the state, for the state can live only at the price of such a mutilation. The divine sentence: "Nothing outside the state,"[7] means, in fact, religiously speaking: nothing shall remain alive of that which is extraneous to the godlike state; everything and everybody shall be victims, so that the state may become a god; there is no life for the state except war. In a free way, the sentence should mean, on the contrary: everything is human, everything is a relationship of human freedom, nothing exists outside human relations, outside the state: therefore, there are no strangers, and hence no victims; there is no other possible reality for the state but peace.

---

7. From Benito Mussolini (and Giovanni Gentile), "The Doctrine of Fascism," in the *Enciclopedia Italiana*, 1932; a summation of the doctrine of totalitarianism.

But for those barren men, who are divorced and severed from sacred aboriginal chaos, there is neither state nor common weal. Nothing is in the state; and therefore peace and war are without meaning: war, for barren reason, is an incomprehensible madness, and peace—a practical and negative ideal, a useless and lifeless absence of war.

The sacrifice of the defeated enemy is a necessity of religious war: hence, the frightfulness of war, which increases in proportion to its sacredness and to the love bestowed upon the national banner. The enemy's blood represents the blood of the idol: the state must bleed in order to live and conquer; to die for one's country is therefore a sacerdotal privilege. War is the business of free men, of citizens, and not of slaves: the warrior class is jealously restricted. Therefore, in times heroic, war is nothing but duels of illustrious champions, contests between military seniors, and the people do not fight, the people only serve under the tents, and carry the burdens, and feed the horses, which are driven by heroes of minor rank. Feudal wars are restricted to the knights, and the peasant troops consist not of fighters but of military servants. Combat service, and the blood which has been shed, are the fount of right, the origin of citizenship and nobility; hence the political strength of the English yeomanry, for instance. The various degrees of power and authority within the state are marked by the various arms: the *hastati*, the *quirites*, the lictors, the archers, etc.[8] The nobleman, in the quiet days of the eighteenth century, did not go out without carrying his useless sword; and the peasant of Southern Italy, even today, never forgets his anarchical brigand-axe, even when he does not go to the woods. For the same reason, officers carry a sword even in time of peace, and they must surrender this symbol when taken prisoners. Military uniform is sacred; it is the vesture of a god. The appearance of a savage warrior, painted white, mottled and monstrous, is enough to put the enemy to flight, because it is a divine apparition. The figure of the warrior must be, as far as possible, an exact image of the idol; so that it may truly take the

---

8. The *hastati* were early Roman legionnaires; the *quirites* were, literally, "spearmen."

idol's place in killing and in dying. Therefore shields and escutcheons carry the divine image and describe, in religious language, the state, its origin and nature. Even modern military uniforms are a reminder of the corresponding national flags and skies and landscapes: in the grey common mimicry, France is sky-blue, Italy green, Germany black and white. The medieval warrior stands in iron armor, locked in its narrowness as in the limits of the feudal domain, plumed with nobility, towering above his shield like a castle above its walls, and with his visor down, forced to silence and pride. The common people's fighters despise the swords, just as they scorn every state-idol; they glory in ignoble weapons, in pitchforks and scythes, in sporting guns, in knives and stones. When they put Justice or Reason upon the altar they sometimes take for a weapon the guillotine, one of the most rationally and legitimately religious of arms: but as long as they are moved by a sacred and free impulse, they need devise no uniforms, for they themselves are not divided from those who are not fighting. With the rebirth of the monster-gods and of the god-machines, our present-day uniforms acquire again a monstrous and picturesque appearance: the typical beastlike shape of the gas mask is a symptom and a proof of the true aspect of our state-idols.

To die in war is a privilege, an indispensable sacrifice cherished by the god of the state. To kill in war is no offence, it is a merit: it is not criminal bloodshed, but the shedding of sacred blood; it is a task of priests and sacrificers. To be killed in war, as a thousand epigraphs point out, is not to die; it means truly to gain immortality, the very immortality of the state, for one dies for the state, instead of the state, under its banners, with its colors. Everywhere, in every time, poetry and mythology have distinguished this death from every other death, and made it the highest ambition, the most dignified end. Even popular tradition gives to such death a form similar to the death of the gods: an Italian war song sings of a dying officer who asks that his body be divided in seven parts; and, for the heroes most admired, a spontaneous legend takes shape, according to which every one of them was killed by a bullet right in the forehead, even if the circumstances of their death were many and various. Only a complete alteration of the state-deities, and the freedoms which result from such a change, allow the Achilles of the *Odyssey* to lament the death of Achilles in the *Iliad*, or enable Horace to tell the story of his own flight, a flight from death heroic.

relicta non bene parmula[9]

Only those who, at war, shed the enemy's blood and their own are able to partake, really and bodily, in the divinity of the state. Never, therefore, are the serfs allowed to touch weapons; and war is preserved, desired, and considered a necessity by those who identify themselves with their own state-idol, war being the only way to preserve both deity and slavery. Continual, but limited war. Savage warriors and feudal lords live only and solely by a war without interruption, which confirms and consecrates their power, a war which allows to increase both the number of slaves and the weight of their chains. But war is limited by the small numbers of fighting men, and, because of its ritual character, by a thousand usages, declarations and ceremonies. The supreme request of those who are not warriors is to gain permission to join the fight, in order to enter the mystery of the state and partake of the hieratic nature of men and citizens.

The gods fight their battles on the shores of the sea, they drive the chariot and wield the spear. A people of serfs stand aside and look on, silent and patient, resigned victims of the god which shall conquer. The rank and file are witnesses of war, as they are witness to the state, through their indifferent servitude. They well know in their hearts that the gods are a necessary evil; and that these gods are all alike, however dissimilar in colors and emblems, in name and appearance, for all of them consist of a ritual mutilation; of a burden which forces every man to bow down—so that instead of getting lost in the infinite blue of the sky, he is forced to remain content with the earth and rejoice in its crops and green grass.

---

9.   "Having indecorously thrown the shield away" (Horace, *Odes* 2.10).

The populace feels the dark terror which gives birth to the gods; it knows only too well the vagueness of its own power, the uncertainty of its own limits; it accepts as unavoidable the religious, hereditary bounds. Bondage upon earth to the gods of the earth, and after death—to the gods of heaven. Freedom seems inconceivable: how can one live a life without ties, and follow a law ever new, a limit equal to infinity? War engenders servitude, the deity's life, and death, the deity's blood. The peasant and serf—no partner, but passive victim—watches the heavy warriors passing through his fields with horses and chariots, and the marauders hard on their heels; and he hides in the woods upon their passage.

The idol-state knows but two fundamental castes: the serfs and the warriors. Both castes are victims, the former sacrificing their bodies to the deity in the hardships and toils of work; the latter—their souls and their blood. They are passive, animal, victims, strange to the idol—or on the contrary, active and sacerdotal, made one with the deity itself. In order not to serve, there is but one way, the way of killing and dying. Therefore the right of fighting is the most coveted right, the only one allowing bodily participation in the divinity of the state. This is why the brave flourish of war stirs up the spirits of youth, pouring some heroism in the citizens' hearts,[10] as if heavenly bugles were sounding liberty eternal. But the sacerdotal image of war is so true and deeply rooted that, even when all men take part in the fighting, they are still considered not as priests, but as servants of the temple—the sacrificer's crown of oak leaves being reserved for the general, while the former slaves turned citizens and soldiers have to be content with the serf's knapsack and the piglike gas mask of the totemic victim. War is a privilege and sacerdotal distinction—thus even in states which proclaim themselves states "of the people," no discipline is conceivable except one that is dictatorial and tyrannical. It is not merely a matter of technique or competence to obey without question one's superiors: it is also a matter of faith. Everything in an

---

10. "Versent quelque héroisme au coeur des citadins" (Charles Baudelaire, "Les Petites Vieilles," in *Les Fleurs du Mal* [1857]).

army is religious: the military language, which consists of identical commands and evocatory formulas, sharing the nature of prayer and magic; the shape of the weapons, which results from a perfect symbolism even more than from a consummate technique; the appearance of uniforms and medals; the sacred enclosures where the flag is kept untouchable and hidden until the religious ceremony of battle, when it is displayed upon the altar in the field; the virtue of hierarchy and discipline, fundamentals of the military religion; the consecrated slaughter of the enemy, and the ritual death of the priests-idols-victims.

The warrior once had the task of being a living holocaust and of conquering for his god the due tribute of enemy slaves. The army's task is a similar one, though performed with greater completeness, whenever the army, instead of remaining a part of and organ of the state (and having therefore to distinguish itself from the servile victims) grows to be the entire state, in its totality. The warrior then becomes a soldier, the privilege of arms becomes military servitude; and it is discipline which keeps the victim and the priest apart. War no longer requires external aims, nor foes to bring into subjection; for it reaches all its aims even without reasons, and without battles: it furnishes the state with servants bearing testimony, through their very delusion, to the state's power, and offers victims whose blood inspires the state with a godlike soul.

The structure of the army is a mirror of the social religion. The hero battles all alone; the paladin rides through vales and woods to find his match among the knights. In the aristocratic states there is a class of warrior noblemen, and to join those who bear arms is one of ambition's highest rewards, worth striving for through civil struggles. Peoples without state-religion, such as the Chinese and the Neapolitans, despise the soldier, almost as if he were a murderer. The decay of state-religiosity turns the privileges into profession: auxiliary troops, mercenaries, make their appearance; the vanquished peoples themselves are turned into soldiers, instead of being made slaves. In times of liberty, if armies are raised in defense against an antiquated institution or surviving foreign idols, the entire people are soldiers, while officers and generals are improvised;

and the casualties, freely accepted, confirm a community which is not afraid, and has no need of self-worship. Here fighting is no longer only a privilege; it is a moral necessity, a duty—and it does not give the fighter a place among either the masters or the servants. In every other case, heroism is religion, and the army is a church. A ground-swell of freedom, rolling through the centuries, unites with the Jacobins' religion of liberty, and raises from the furrows a people in arms. Through the mere memory of this enthusiasm and of this faith, they sweep on, to the very limits of the world.

Later on, a purely juridical liberalism (the true "religion" of liberty) had to draw the distinction between what is duty and what is right in the bearing of arms for the state's service; and, as the terms of liberalism were entirely functional, it was no longer possible to speak of military privilege, or honor; or of military slavery or sacrifice—but only of military *service*, which is an obligation for all alike, and is accepted by all as a voluntary burden. However, in this juridically unimpeachable form, the army, while belonging to everybody, remained nevertheless what it was before: a church, with its own ritual, its own castes, its sacred emblems and sacred discipline; in short, a state, a god, in contradiction with abstract liberalism, and even more so—with such concrete liberties as could live under the veil of this abstraction. The First World War hurled to their death those ambiguous citizens' armies—and many soldiers deemed themselves to be fighters for freedom who after having overcome, through war and blood, every social and historical difference and every servitude, were uniting at last with the entire state in a free community of people. Others felt their participation to be a truly ritual one; they slaughtered victims, enjoyed it, and rightly believed that they alone—the sacrificers—could form the divine state; and these became, forever, the veteran fighters. Still others died, or resigned themselves to serve. However, the fact that the entire people is called to arms without becoming the entire state, and that they must contribute to the war their bodies and their blood, while taking part in the state only through a juridical fiction such as a delegation of powers or plebiscitary approval, is nothing but a paradox, an evident contradiction. Universal participation in the ritual of war should abolish servitude and state-idolatry, and it should serve therefore as the visible sign of human liberty. In consequence, wherever state-idolatry, inherited from the fathers or born anew, was strongest, there had to be a bolstering up of military discipline,—that is, a distinction between two different kinds of fighters: the priests and the servants of the temple. There was established a voluntary militia, a privileged warrior caste, with special arms, and uniforms and colors (black, the sacred color of death) and banners. Wars requiring the people's intervention were avoided as much as possible, and it was attempted to wage limited, heroic wars, with a few chosen forces, while leaving the peasant at his plough, away from the weapons, as in the days of the barbarians. Above all, it was attempted to identify the entire state with the army, and to confer upon the army the characteristics of a church, with an ever growing internal military servitude, and a new flowering of ritual. Military religion here becomes identical with the religion of the state: thus only is it possible to wage universal war without giving up slavery. The goose step is an absolute necessity for a servile and churchlike army—and this step is certainly no more strange than the kneelings and bowings and thousand picturesque ceremonies of countless religious cults, official or private. Its ritual virtue resides, precisely, in its absurdity and uselessness. It is a walking in foreign language, a kind of sacred armed dance—just as prayer amounts to speaking in the language of mystery.

Those who believe in the necessity of state-idolatry, and therefore of slavery and war, are compelled—in order to involve their entire people in war while keeping slavery untouched—to transform the entire state into an army, and the army into a church. Should the people be warlike, the state would fall from its divine altars. War must be waged not by a free people in arms, but by a mass of serfs organized into an army. The idols of state and army, of the machine and organization must coincide: so that the gods of the state may live, war must be continuous, not interrupted by the semblance of peace; it must be total, organized and mechanical. The warrior's severance from war must be made manifest, war must become inhuman, out of reach for the single fighting man, the performance of symbolic monsters and of incomprehensible bureaucratic agencies. In short, on the one hand the entire people must be organized into a churchlike army so that slavery may survive, and on the other hand war must be suffered and borne, but not really fought, by a people of slave soldiers, in order to prevent the privilege of freedom, which belongs to the warrior, from becoming universal and abolishing the worship of the state. It is no easy task to fulfill these two requirements: therefore, on every side, there is little determination to wage war, and, after war has started, to fight it in a thorough and bloody fashion. The people's wars engender liberty; and liberty makes every war futile. But state-idols live only upon wars; and they need peoples to wage them. And this makes necessary the modern and military organization of the state.

War is a rite, and as such needs no justification. Or rather, war is most efficient and divinity-breeding when it seems absurd and incomprehensible to reason. *Justified* wars, those that are waged in order to protect one's own life or one's own soul, are not religious wars, and therefore have no idolatrous efficiency. Only unjustifiable wars create power and life for the idols of the state. A prayer, to be efficacious, must have little meaning; war, to be useful for the state-divinity, must have no justification. Victims, in whatever religion, need to be perfect: if animals, they should be sound in body; if humans, they should have no faults, or defects, or diseases; the true victim is pure and innocent. Some people are still of the opinion that war is a violent means to solve definite material questions, which, of course, would be solved even better around a conference table, but which, unfortunately, may be decided quite legitimately by a trial of strength, provided that every other means has proved impracticable. These people believe therefore in the possibility of arbitrating disputes and they deplore the bombing of open cities or the sinking of ships without warning. But they forget that there can be no more reason for war than there is for prayer: that the only reason for war is the lack of reason (for, wherever there is reason, there is no war); that true and efficient wars are only those which have no justification; and that only innocent victims can serve as divine nourishment, and be palatable to the gods.

"Reasonable wars" and peoples' armies belong to a purely juridical conception of liberty. But true liberty, not the merely institutional freedoms, knows nothing of war, for it has already won all wars, and knows nothing of armies, for it has destroyed them all; and whenever liberty has to fight in order to defend itself against renascent gods and resurgent armies, it means that freedom was not entirely true and not entirely free. Every war waged by liberty is an interior struggle, an enrichment, an increase of peace, a civil war: that civil war which never has a beginning and never shall have an end, just as the chain of birth and death has no beginning and no end. Expressions of the selfsame pharisaism are the conventions for the humanization of war, the protection of the civilian population, and so forth. The milder customs of war derived merely from the waning and decline of the religious sense of war, and from the transformation of certain warlike ventures into purely commercial undertakings, such as colonial wars, the conquest of oilfields, mines, etc.—as well as from the existence of a real religion of humanity and abstract liberty, in opposition to the religion of state. But war cannot be *humanized*, because it is divine. The prisoner must be sacrificed. Civilians, women and children may be spared and forgotten by the warrior, who does not grant them the privilege of dying; but wherever there are no true warriors any more—merely armed and servile masses—there cannot be any privileges nor distinctions. Women and children are part of the mass, and to spare them is a sacrilege.

War weighs down upon the masses, although they take part in it, as a tremendous obscurity, as a phenomenon of nature, indifferent and mysterious. The cold stars of winter glitter in their familiar abodes in the cloudless sky; but from the four corners of heaven there swoop down, like angels or demons, the wings of the bombers. The howl of the city's sirens, in the gray dawn of the roofs, is the voice of war, and its sacred language. A machine is speaking, a machine is fighting, and the man inside is no longer a warrior or really a man: he has merged with the machine and assumed its indifference, its certainty; together with it, he has turned again into a double monster, a beast-like monster of remote antiquity. A new ambiguity is taking shape, a mechanical and sportive association of power and servitude. A thousand new Orions, evil and smiling, are out to hunt through the great forest of heaven. At the roar of their horns the dragons of old awaken, and blood, ready to be shed, throbs violently in every heart, which is filled with ancient terrors and the most ancient hopes.

Testa di vitello scuoiata (Skinned calf's head, 1935)

Every autonomy, every act of creation, is, by its very nature, outside this law, inimical to the state, a sacrilege.

7 / Mass

More ancient than any memory, more vague than any hope, more remote than birth itself, there dwells in every heart an unlimited darkness. Like the shadow of a body at the rising or setting of the sun, this darkness narrows or spreads out with the rise or decline of each person—always, however, persisting. Behind all luminous actions and thoughts there is this leisure of the world, this black margin of eternal passivity, this necessary nothingness, this bottomless contradiction from which all things originate, measureless and without termination. It is an absolute with no limits, and therefore with no existence, like its opposite—finiteness absolute—which, if we may trust the philosophers, is a self-contradictory concept. But this non-existence is the negative limit of every living individuation; it is the chaotic condition of every birth; the hollow cave of love. It is shapeless matter, heavy with all weight, lacking all quality, and full of every passive potential.

Bakers call "mass" the dough before it is divided into loaves to become bread in the oven; for metalfounders "mass" is the melted metal before it is cast into the mold; for physicists—that which in a body is neither shape, nor size, nor quality, but indeterminate matter. Mass appears to every individual as a "not me," unavoidable though non-existent, and which for every physical body is a non-quality, the negative origin of all qualities, and constitutes, in the field of human relationship, a non-state, a formlessness, from which arises by contradiction every organism of state. It is indeterminate human material, which is one, and therefore incapable of relationship, although it holds within itself, within its non-existence, all possible future relations. The mass is nothingness, it is sleep and anarchical oneness; it is the negative image of the state. From its infinite indifference arise men and states, but every birth, every nation, is a fracture of the mass, a decrease of that shadow which constitutes both their origin and their limit.

Its equally non-existent opposite, anarchical multiplicity, the impossibility of the state, is finiteness absolute, the abstract individual, and old age. History is nothing but the eternal venture of the human mass in its laborious endeavor to determine itself, to resolve itself into state, poetry, liberty, or to abscond into religion, rite, custom; and of the continuous resurgence of the mass from the drying-up of the states and the crystallization of religions. The mass dwells in each of us, hidden in a depth far deeper than conscience and memory, for it is itself the sacred limit of memory and conscience. In the great individual body of a people, mass is pure matter, outside historical conscience and recollection. Mass, in a people, is everything which has no shape, and which strives obscurely to separate, to segregate, and to originate as a person and a state. A mass, therefore, is not the people, not even its lower part, the plebe, nor any social class in particular; but it is the indeterminate crowd, which tries, with the anguish of the mute, to express itself and achieve existence. The characters of Faulkner are a mass—human beings of a still mutable shape, which could, materially, take on monstrous forms; they try in vain to tell themselves apart from their fellows, under the crude light of August which equalizes all things in its harshness; driven by an obscurely common blood, they attempt, in a furious rebellion, to break away from the undifferentiated matter out of which they have been arbitrarily shaped—like sunken bubbles which rise again towards the surface of the sea. In the swarming of the crowd, they cannot really talk and establish human relations, because none of them has any limits, and none of them is yet really born. Their expressions are outcries, killings, prayers—and the atmosphere is one of continual fright, caused by that which is happening and by that which can never happen, and by the incomprehensibility of the continuous attempt.

In every origin there is this formless humanity; and it appears again whenever human intercourse becomes inaccessible, and similar to a mysterious idol perceived by men not as a creation and relationship, but as a destiny. Destiny throws all men together into a common aboriginal equality, and, being indifferent, makes them undifferentiated again.

War, waged by men, but severed from men and incomprehensibly divine, a necessary sacrifice to the divinity of the state, not only disrupts certain definite relations existing between men, but tends to bring men back to that undifferentiation which precedes relationship. A law of death, inhuman like nature, rules everybody's lot; and chance (a chance which men have caused, but which is a mystery to every single man) chooses among them and destroys them. Blood, this liquid shapeless life, covers the earth as a sign of aboriginal community. Physical pain, the suffering of the body, which is an equal burden upon all men, is a daily occurrence, awaited for the morrow. Names are forgotten; a uniform conceals everybody alike in an invisible gray fog. A cloud covers the face of the earth, and in it mankind dissolves, before dying, as if it were a huge indistinct body, wounded and painful, which hides its head and closes its eyes, and nevertheless lives on and spreads like immortal water. Great wars, by themselves, engender the mass: they turn again into a mass which was already determined, and confer a shapeless life to things already crystallized. Every man leaves his house, abandons his own world which was unique to him, merges with all his fellowmen, and after losing everything which made him a person, arrives to that which is indistinguishably common: blood and death.

Great concentrations of people, large cities, also develop the mass and create it anew. An isolated family, a village, a town of moderate size, do not overtax man's ability to observe and understand: they force him to make a choice, to determine himself by requiring from him a total contribution, not a merely mechanical specialization. But the big city is incomprehensible: one cannot grasp it at a glance, for it lives its own life, the life of a gigantic body through which there runs a blood made of a million unconscious human creatures; and these humans are all alike, living side by side without knowing each other, lost in a boundless resemblance. The city grows at its own margins, like an enormous expanding protoplasm. The suburbs have a tragic appearance, dusty and indeterminate. Vacant lots are covered with fences and wild grass, unexpected walls spring up through the meadows, in the squalid uncertainty of a city which has ceased to be bountiful. This shapeless landscape does not display the feeling of things human, or of the things of nature, but only the urge of a life uncertain and equal everywhere, the life of a generical humanity, unable to express itself through the artistry of the buildings or through the orderliness of the fields, and kept out of both, waiting at the door, in patience or in rage. Streets and houses have no definite ending, they only border upon stretches of land no less indefinite: it is the place of a people without history or memories, uprooted from any determination, and with none of the precise colors of a particular hope. The dread of cities hardly arises from the contemporaneity of times upon the paved squares of townships rich in history, trodden by countless dissimilar generations; it does arise from the mystery of boroughs where the silent human crowds are encamped, who have not yet begun to live, and to whom all history is a future.

Where the gods live, men must have an end and hide themselves and find again a contact with their origins. War and city are divine places, where men re-enter the mass. Even work is deified, becoming technique and organization. The factory, grown gigantic, is not understandable to those who live off it, for they are no longer participants but merely tools. Technique, the art of human workmanship and invention, becomes a secret technology, no longer art, but magic. And organization destroys every living organism by imposing upon it its own extraneous divinity. Where there is an organism, there cannot be organization. The latter presupposes shapelessness, and creates shapelessness, to give it a divinely arbitrary order. The works of man, which also constitute a language made of objects, a poetry of things, are not possible any more in a world anonymous, a world without a name, without the gift of speech, unable to express itself, which may labor and slave and pray, but not create. Therefore things become mechanical, they become religious and reproducible expressions, works divine.

Arisen from the mass, and creating the mass, the gods of war, of the city, of the machine, of organization, are nothing but particular aspects, singular expressions and attributes of a greater god, which alone is born of the mass and lives upon the mass—the idol of the state. Mass is infinite repetition, infinite uniformity, infinite impossibility of correlation, absolute impossibility of state—as well as sacred terror before this immense powerlessness, irresistible urge for determination and for unobtainable freedom. Wherever human relations are being established, the mass ends, and man is born, as well as the state. But where the mass persists, with its vague burden and mortal fright, a religion of protection and salvation substitutes for the impossible state some divine symbol, and shapes the mass itself, the non-existent and anguished mass, into an idol which hides it and represents it. The divinity of the mass and that of the state do coincide; the two idols have a single appearance: totality. The dread of absolute and indistinct passiveness, and the dread of liberty, engender, from opposite sides, one single religion: the mass state. As a reality, this concept is contradictory: the state begins where the mass ends; but as a religious expression, the state can be only of the mass. The sacrifices which engender the god and make him true, are, as we have said before, an alienation of the god's very nature; in the idolatry of the state, it is the state itself which has to be sacrificed; that is, for the idol to live, men must turn into mass and come to naught through undifferentiation. Therefore, idol-states need the crowd, and create the crowd, and tend, in conformity with their nature, to suppress every personality and every relationship. Where there is attained, not only juridically, but also in fact, an equality which amounts to shapelessness, and an external justice which amounts to common death, the state is truly divine.

There is no more tongue; the mass, by itself ineffable and silent, truly may find expression only through the state, that is through the religious language of ritual and prayer. Therefore, instead of the spontaneous political and poetical speech, made of innumerable gestures and words, and of relations ever renewed, there appears a sacred language, the language of mass-manifestation, upon the public squares, below the altars of the tribune, in which, as in the classic prayers, the worshipping crowd contents itself with rhythmical replies, such as the *Amen*, the *Ora pro nobis*, the *Kyrie eleison*, and thus feels liberated, as a partaker of the divinity. Wherever the mass is really anonymous, incapable of naming itself and speaking, the sacred language of the state replaces the names, which have lost their meaning, by its own religious and symbolic names: these are numbers, tickets, banners, arm-bands, uniforms, badges, insignia, medals, identification cards, ritual expressions of the fundamental idolized uniformity, and of the idolized uniform organization. Where the spoken word is made impossible by the very nature of the mass, it is useless to speak about the freedom of speech; the law's intervention may at most sanction the non-existence of free speech, and prevent its possible beginning. Those places where there is speech, the high and low Parnassi of political poetry, solemn or vulgar, the parliaments, debating societies and public meetings, the *salons*, and shops and cafés, lose their functions of giving expression to social relations and disappear. Mass-manifestations cannot be expressive: there is no place in them for diversity and thought—only for the oneness of action; not action as freedom, but solely action as passivity, necessity, nature, the weight of undivided numbers: the plebiscite. Poetical language is impossible, and so are art and culture: they must be replaced by religious language, by the ritual of arms, by a certainty capable of repetition. The cities' architecture becomes uniform: to build is no longer to express an ever different personality, but to symbolize an indeterminate power: and therefore, vagueness of feeling must be banished from the symbol, precisely because the symbolized passion—passivity—is indistinct and uncertain. Art grows into monotonous repetition, into a litany, or else it becomes a desperate and impossible groping for freedom, nostalgia or hope. The sense is lost of living relations, for they are replaced by a single relationship, which is symbolic and arbitrary.

Cities grow by peripheral progression, like unicellular organisms, and spread through the countryside like a shapeless liquid. Culture, which consists everywhere and at all times of a universal and absolute ability to make distinctions, has no meaning at all, in the indistinctness of the mass. And thus, instead of culture, there stands its religious equivalent, a totalitarian, arbitrary will of confusion, which expands, as matter does, by propagation, and which is valid not as a value, but as a weight: *propaganda*, the culture of the masses.

Propaganda is always religious, it is always *Propaganda fides*: to believe in the idol is not to think, but to adore; it is practical, not poetical expression. The state does not speak through words, but through acts of will, like a god; its language is law, and all law is religious; for it is not the inner norm of a singular deed, but the external and arbitrary norm of any possible action. The mass cannot be an organism, which is a moral law, an intimately autonomous unit; the mass can only be an *organization*, that is an external, transcendent differentiation, born of a power extraneous to the mass, which passively persists. The state's existence resides in its external law, a law efficient and idol-breeding precisely in the measure in which it is external and arbitrary. Every autonomy, every act of creation, is, by its very nature, outside this law, inimical to the state, a sacrilege.

Without the externality of law, the mass would remain immobile, the divine state non-existent. It is necessary therefore that law should be present continually, at every moment of life, (and any distinction between private and public life is meaningless), that law should manifest itself by the evident arbitrariness of its interdictions, commands, and obligatory ceremonies, by the religious solemnity of its ritual, by a spectacular display of uniforms, by the heaviness of the punishments it inflicts.

Since the mass has no limits, its state-equivalent, in its symbolical and hierarchic preciseness, is an idol of unlimited power, to which nothing may be extraneous, and the mystery of which is absolute. To this idol everything must be sacrificed—both freedom and blood. Its necessary rites are total slavery and continuous war. The theory concerning the mass-state finds therefore a most perfect expression in this law, truly sublime in its precision, which commands "to believe, to obey, to fight."[1] Where the mass is sacred and the state divine, one can neither create nor speak, but only believe and pray. Every autonomous action is sacrilegious and deadly to the idol: obedience alone is required. Furthermore, blood being the soul of the mass, bloody sacrifice is inevitable and providential: only war eternal engenders the gods.

Thus, the mass creates the idol-state; and the idol-state, in its turn, brings mankind back to the primeval condition of a mass. It is the dread of human identity, the impotent need of freedom which forms the religion of the state. Formless man knows nothing outside himself, and therefore cannot know his own self. Infinite repetition of a sacred identical darkness does not amount to multiplicity and life. For the One, even if monotonously repeated, there cannot be Another one: therefore no relation, no activity no word, no love is possible—only an immense infernal anxiety, and an unconscious striving towards a painful birth. An otherness has to be created: the religious symbol of man's shapeless unity, the godlike state, is appointed to serve as the Other, as the liberating element. But, as the pure passivity of the mass is a non-existence, so also the pure form of the state is no less futile. One does not talk with one's own reflection in the mirror, and the love of the seventeenth-century Narcissus is not love, but death. The image on the water's surface, the godlike state, is really nothing other than the undifferentiated mass—both identical with it and hostile. The identity between mass and divine state is absolute: both are the selfsame non-existence, viewed as a pure matter or as a pure form. This is the deeper meaning of the prayer, so many times repeated, with such faith, by millions of identical beings moved by a same unconscious inspiration: *Ein Volk, ein Reich, ein Fuehrer*.[2] If the people

---

1. "Credere, obeddire, combattere!" was one of Mussolini's many exhortations to the Italians and could be found painted and stenciled in public places in fascist Italy.
2. "One People, one Empire, one Leader!" was often chanted by Hitler's adoring crowds in Nazi Germany.

are a materially indistinct unit, that is, if they are not a people, but a mass, the state is also a unit, formal and arbitrary, a totalitarian idol; and the leader, the one and only leader, shall be truly, materially, exactly the same as the mass, that mass which he does not represent, but symbolizes: for indeed, the symbols of the gods are the gods themselves.

Pure mass is a non-existence; a shapeless death. The pure, divine state is impossible too—a void death. In all eternity, from the one death and the other, freedom and poetry are born; and the mass lives only by the presence of both, and by their continual opposition, which is the continual sacrifice of men to the gods. As long as there are ten righteous men, the city is spared; as long as there remains a single righteous one, the city avoids destruction; only when this one good man is gone, does Sodom perish in confusion. The state-idol can stand only as long as it faces a stranger: a foe which is necessary, which will have to be perpetually expelled, and perpetually discovered again—a providential victim.

Night's darkness dwells in the depth of man: upon the works of man the sun is shining; and when the sun has set, a few stars, or a glimmer in the night, are testimony to the coming morrow. The area of shadow is large or small, according to men and according to the times, and that which is obscure, sacred and shameful is covered by the gods. The dread of human relationship can never be absolute; the word never entirely silenced, the prayer never the only expression; slavery never complete, war never without peace to follow, the state never completely totalitarian. But when the formless extends to a great part of the soul, when sacred terror weighs on the heart, we recognize the power of the state-idol by the sacrifices from which it springs, and by the quality of the holocaust. The god truly reveals himself in the bowels of his dead: divination is, literally, the knowledge of things divine through the bloody language of the victims. The hidden wisdom of sacred things, the true knowledge of religious history, is written in sacrifices and martyrdom. Bowing down to watch the tepid blood which gushes forth from the open bodies, we shall find in it the very face of the god, distinguishable from any other god by the shape of the wounds inflicted.

The sacred history of the world is a history of willing servitude, of tortures, punishments and mutilations, of interdictions, expulsions and ritual killings, of slaughter and intolerance, of prisons and exiles. The myriad state-idols are recognized in the myriad victims; each one of these bears upon itself the imprint of the priest, as a witness to mortal faith, describes by the pain it suffers the shape and power of its particular divinity.

Colomba (Dove, 1935)

Man, in order to become a god, drives himself out of his own self, expels, exiles and kills himself; in vain does he strive throughout eternity to reach again his paradise lost, by consecrating victims in his stead, by driving them out, by exiling and killing them, so that he may not die, so that he may become at least a god, if he may not any longer remain a man.

8 / Sacred History

The myth of the Scriptures is the mysterious tale, the sacred history of man between one death and the other, through the path of religion and liberty. And the venture begins, quite rightly, by an exile, by the loss of Paradise. What is it, however, this sin from which originates every alienation, every enmity, every pain, every death? The myth, taken as a symbol, may have a thousand meanings, all of them equally true: disobedience, pride, lack of faith—and even sexual lust, according to the vulgar interpretation, which is the Milanese and the Dutch one, the Ambrosian and Beverlandian. All the symbolic meanings are equally true: but the letter of the myth is clear, and includes them all in its truth.

The sin of Adam consists of having partaken of a fruit which gives the knowledge of good and evil. But how could there be sin before the knowledge of good and evil? And how could there be, prior to this knowledge, a prohibition which it was sinful to infringe? Or could it be that the birth of moral conscience is in itself a sin? What is the meaning of the tree, and the serpent with its eternal flattery? What is the sin that engenders death?

A man lived in the garden, and he was free, for he was "a living soul." The word dwelt in him: he alone gave things a name. Moral conscience dwelt in him: he knew that the fruits were good, he knew that his woman was "bone of his bones, and flesh of his flesh," he knew that "a man shall leave his father and his mother,

and shall cleave unto his wife, and they shall be one flesh."[1] Passion
was in him, "for deep sleep" was upon him. He was "naked": there
was in him an infinite indetermination, but he was "not ashamed,"
he had no sacred dread of it, because this indeterminateness was
at the same time a determination, and nakedness covered itself
without need of being hidden. Thus, he was a man, solely and totally man, and lived in the freedom which was the happiness of the
garden. Every action was an act of liberty, for it contained in itself
its own norm; every work was creative: man was in the garden "to
dress it and to keep it," and work was as happy and easy as breath-
ing; every word was a word of poetry, identical with its object and of
absolute value: "and whatsoever Adam called every living creature,
that was the name thereof."[2] He was not alone: with him there
was a woman, made of his rib, and he lived with her, and with the
beasts, and with the trees, and with the lights in the firmament; he
was not alone, for he was not separated from them; although an
autonomous being, he was at one with all; and because he was not
alone, not separated, neither he nor they knew death. His death-
lessnes was no unlimited extension within a passing time, but eternal contemporaneity of every moment: for this time was not outside himself, nor outside the garden of the world, but concentrated
in the eternal liberty of every instant. He was entirely one with
the earth of which he had been formed, and the "breath of life"
that was breathed into his nostrils may have been nothing but the
mist which "went up from the earth, and watered the whole face
of the garden."[3] Could it be that Adam was the man made upon
the sixth day, in the image and after the likeness of God[4]—or was
he another one? The sacred book does not explain it; but certainly
he was a man, not God, and his freedom was human, not divine,
like his conscience, like the eternal time and place of his life. He
dwelt in the human land of liberty, for within him the earth and the

---

1. Genesis 2.19.
2. Genesis 2.6.
3. Genesis 2.6.
4. Genesis 1.26.

spirit—his own particular nature, and universal value—were indissolubly united. The garden of the world was Adam himself—and
within him there could be no distinction of good and evil, for evil
was possible only in an *outside*, in going out of one's own self, and
out of one's absolute freedom. Adam was entirely man and the entire man, and in man there is no place for sin.

But the fruit of the tree in the midst of the garden was the fruit
of sin, (which is at one and the same time knowledge and punish-
ment), for it was the fruit of divinity. One who eats of this fruit
shall be "as a god"—he shall separate and distinguish himself, and
remove himself from the garden and the world, and look at them
from the outside. Thus do good and evil originate, and "the knowledge of good and evil"; thus ends the freedom of moral law that
is innate in things, and thus starts the serfdom of the external, of
the religious law. The eyes of Adam saw the world from the inside:
they did not need to be opened in order to see. Once the fruit
had been eaten, his eyes were "opened" upon an outside world,
which is the world of separation. Man becomes a god, in the effort of self-individuation and of severance from things, and looks
even at himself as at a thing, for—having made himself a god—he
is separated forever from his own self. But this thing, at which he
is looking from the outside, has no shape, for it is at one with the
world, and cannot be really seen from the outside, no outside having any existence whatsoever. Therefore this thing is naked—that
is sacred and shameful. The eyes of Adam are opened to behold
something frightful, something which ought to be covered and hidden, and dismissed. The time of liberty, which was real time, and
therefore time eternal, becomes, when seen from the outside, a
material time flowing into death: and thus the tree is mortal, and
Adam must revert to dust. The interior law of freedom becomes the
external law of sin; confusion comes in, and separation, and idolatry and sacrifice. The Lord God, who intervenes and expels Adam,
as also the tempter snake, is nothing but a poetical impersonation,
a hypostasis of man himself: indeed, expulsion is nothing else than
the eating of the fruit of divinity, and temptation is sin itself. Having put his law and poetry and life outside himself, Adam dwells

no more in freedom, he is no longer in the garden. His love is no longer love, but amorous tyranny and servitude: "thy desire shall be to thy husband, and he shall rule over thee."[5] Begetting ceases to be a bliss, and becomes an effort and a pain, torn between power and separation: "in sorrow shalt thou bring forth." Creation turns into fatigue and slavery: "in the sweat of thy face shalt thou eat bread."[6] The world, instead of true, is symbolic—monsters and idols are born; the serpent becomes a worm, and life a war, ending in death. Perpetuity which would be reached by eating of the tree of life, could not be the eternity of each instant, could not be freedom, but a divine timelessness, which develops to no end—the non-existent time of the gods. Thus, the tree of good and evil is but the external law—separation, idolatry. Therefrom does sacred history begin: man, in order to become a god, drives himself out of his own self, expels, exiles and kills himself; in vain does he strive throughout eternity to reach again his paradise lost, by consecrating victims in his stead, by driving them out, by exiling and killing them, so that he may not die, so that he may become at least a god, if he may not any longer remain a man. His idolatrous death continues through the generations and times, until a god has become man—that is, until again the moral law has taken the place of external law, and freedom the place of tyranny, and heavenly Jerusalem the place of earthly Babylon. Until in man every distinction has been abolished: "There is neither Jew nor Greek, there is neither bond nor free, there is neither male or female; for ye are all one."[7] If the law is not sin, "by the works of the law shall no flesh be justified . . . for through the law cometh the knowledge of sin."[8] There can be neither freedom nor justice as long as the law resides outside things, in divine estrangement.

But the coming of Christ is also a myth, like the sin of Adam: and in reality fall and redemption are eternal and ever present.

---

5. Genesis 3.16.
6. Genesis 3.19.
7. Galatians 3.28.
8. Romans 3.20.

Redemption cannot happen once and forever, any more than sin occurred once and for all the beginning of time. A ceaseless fall and a ceaseless renascence make up history: and when liberation becomes religion, then liberation is useless. "For if righteousness is through the law, then Christ is dead in vain," says Paul.[9] Sin, therefore, is man's inability to be free and to give a norm unto himself; it is the search after a law of eternal certitude, a transmutation of liberty into a religious symbol, the fear of God, and accordingly—the fear of self, that self which man has turned into a god. For this particular god the world becomes transcendent, and thus incomprehensible and full of fright: everything turns into an idol and requires sacrifice, everything becomes a temple which hides a sacred being. Original sin, the one and only sin, is separation, the religion of man. Man becomes god and therefore victim—and to be god, he must separate from himself, leave the garden, and shed his brother's blood. He must be a tyrant and a slave, and render inimical and strange his own work and his own love, and tear apart body and spirit, and live in anguish, under a yoke, only to shed his own blood upon the altar. He must put the word outside the things, and life outside life; but "the word is nigh thee, in thy mouth and in thy heart."[10]

Separation, despair, idolatry, are found in all times, and never had a beginning—and freedom, as life itself, is always present. Sacred history puts sin at the beginning of time, for time in its external development is sin itself, and before sin it did not exist. Liberty, the paradise regained, is placed at the end of time. If at the start there is exile, then at the end there is apocalypse, Revelation, a mysterious tale where everyone may find, clearly expressed, his own peculiar story; the second and final narration of Adam's sin, and of the return to the garden, which can only happen through the death of death, through the end of separation, of law, of idolatry, of slavery, and of symbolic substitution. The sin which has to end is man's worship of a thing human, of a beast-like idol, which is an

9. Galatians 2.21.
10. Romans 10.8.

heraldic animal, a monster well adored, a state-religion, war and slavery. It is the serpent, the red dragon, the beast coming up out of the sea, to which the dragon "gave his power, and his throne, and great authority."[11] This beast utters great things and blasphemies, in religious language, and leads people into captivity, and kills men with the sword. It is the other beast coming up out of the earth, which deceives them that dwell on the earth into making and worshipping images, and brings it about "that as many as should not worship the image of the beast should be killed";[12] "and all, the small and the great, and the rich and the poor, and the free and the bond, that there be given them a mark on their right hand, or upon their forehead; and that no man should be able to buy or to sell, save he that hath the mark, even the name of the beast or the number of his name" (which is "the number of a man: six hundred and sixty and six").

It is the great harlot, "that great city, which reigneth over the kings of the earth"[13] and sitteth upon many waters, of "peoples, and multitudes, and nations, and tongues,"[14] and upon the beast, which is a king, of scarlet color, full of blasphemies; and which is drunk with the blood of saints and of prophets, and of all those who have been killed upon earth; "and upon her forehead was a name written: Mystery."[15] Babylon the great shall be destroyed, the city of slaughter and slavery, of mystery and religion. The new paradise, the heavenly Jerusalem, is liberty regained. "And I saw no temple therein: for the Lord God Almighty and the Lamb are the temple of it."[16] The city has no mystery, it is of "pure gold, as it were transparent glass . . . And the city had no need of the sun, neither of the moon to shine in it,"[17]—for the city itself is light, and there is an end to that separation which needs to be lit from outside. No more

---

11. Revelation 13.2.
12. Revelation 13.15.
13. Revelation 17.18.
14. Revelation 17.15.
15. Revelation 17.5.
16. Revelation 21.22.
17. Revelation 21.23.

enclosures and limits: the gates shall in no wise be shut. No more darkness, or light of the law, for "there shall be no night there; and they need no candle, neither light of sun; for the Lord God giveth them light; and they shall reign for ever and ever,"[18]—that is, in a time found again, where there is no before and no after, no day and no night, but where every moment is eternal.

That the poetical, and so truthful story (true only in the ever repeated, infinite experience) of Paradise lost, Redemption and Apocalypse, the story of the rise of human religion, of its liberation and of its ending, has been taken literally and has become a dogma, a law, a religion—is added proof of the tale's profundity and of the truth of its interpretation. For men, incapable of liberty—who cannot stand the terror of the sacred that manifests itself before their open eyes—must turn to mystery, must hide and worship as a dark symbol, the very *revelation*, the shining light of truth.

La Baule
September–December 1939

---

18. Revelation 22.5.

Fear of Painting

Autoritratto (Self-portrait, 1935)

"Paintings are mythical landscapes of the soul . . . and cannot be without intricate, pathless woods, without swamps, without this idle and nocturnal tedium."

A polyphonic chorus of screams and lamentations, of obscure and violent voices; a foreign land inhabited by monsters, of frightening and mysterious images; a time without happiness, without hope, full of defenses; the bloody viscera of an unfamiliar world, laid bare to an enemy sun; all of this, moreover, here, not far away, not outside, but within, just beneath the reflective surface of the soul, under the gaze of a Narcissus troubled at the contemplation of the waters from which he was born—oh painting of our time, I invoke you, oracle of the future, whoever hopes to meditate upon thee must wonder whether he should employ the language of mathematics or, instead, launch into an impassioned panegyric, dispense an epigram or deliver a funeral eulogy, or should he limit himself to gazing upon you, upon your parlous heaving swells, in the hope of attaining some distant, future shore? Whatever the case, whatever the stance of the soul, one's eye penetrates the depths, to the very boundaries of humanity, the lands of listless misery and the most overblown pride—down, down, down, into the elementary and primeval shadows of the Fear of Being.

Because contemporary painting—which begins with Cézannian multiplicity, which shines with desperate energy in Picasso, and which is extinguished, its Capital having fallen, with the realization of its prophecies—has been the divining mirror of the crisis of man and the world: the oracle, mysterious in its simple clarity, of a mortal danger.

The sense of existence as creation, of the identification of man with the world, of every relation as an act of love, turns every mark, every sign, into painting. Freedom creates and sustains human passions: life is like a tree swollen with sap; rich with a happy fullness in which there is place, without contradiction, even for sorrow and anguish and death. The individual is a work of art: the place of all possible relations; he has therefore no limits if not infinite. But for the limited individual, incapable and fearful of existence and freedom, passions don't exist, the world becomes extraneous: it is truly, as the poet said:

Un monde dont je suis absent.[1]

Forced to live in and accept a world from which we are absent, we are therefore absent and estranged from ourselves as well, enwrapped in solitude, no passion is granted us except that of terror. The primordial and fundamental terror, the fear of the world, of life, of freedom, of man: the Fear of Painting. The world, emptied of us, is refilled for us with monsters: man himself becomes a

---

1. "A world in which I am absent" (Paul Éluard, "Giorgio De Chirico," in *Oeuvres complètes* [Paris: Gallimard, 1968], 1:144):

Giorgio De Chirico

A wall denounces another wall
And the shadows defend me from my timid shadow
O tower of my love surrounding my love
My silence turns the walls white

What do you defend? Sky unfeeling and clear,
Trembling you sheltered me. The prominent light
In the sky is no longer the mirror of the sun
But the stars of day among green leaves.

The memory of those who spoke without knowing,
Masters of my weakness. And I have replaced them
With eyes of love and hands too loyal
To depopulate a world from which I am absent.
—1924

Translated by Tom Hibbard, *The Drunken Boat* 3, no. 4 (Winter 2003), http://www.thedrunkenboat.com/Éluardeng.html.

Narciso (1965)

"The goat-boy Narcissus, not yet existentially differentiated from the swirling waters of chaos, risks a mortal danger in identification without distance."

monster to himself, because he is absent from himself. The word, love of ideas and things, can no longer bind us to that which is irremediably torn asunder; we can only symbolically seek defense and certainty. Painting is no longer creative expression, but magic, an instrument of impossible salvation. The fear of the desert of the isolated soul is the meaning of contemporary painting: its objects are not living men or things, but idols.

Man yields neither to the world nor himself: pictorial styles, which are not those of just any scholastic tradition, but the consensus of things and the artificer, no longer have any value. With every relationship ended, what ideal perspective can bind things together? They are all identical in their impenetrability. Every perspective becomes an empty scheme or non-sense. And if the sky becomes empty and black before our eyes, the light will be estranged as an object.

La lumière en relief
sur le ciel qui n'est plus le miroir du soleil.[2]

And the shadow will no longer be the hollow model of living forms, nor a drama of passion, nor feminine maternal caress, but obscurity where our terror hides.

Et l'ombre me defend de mon ombre peureuse.[3]

And color will detach itself from forms and each of the indissoluble elements of pictorial expression will be isolated and lose every tie with the others, and become itself object of incomprehensible fear: and reason will take another path from meaning; and the passages from one to the other moment will become mechanical and symbolic. For men, frightened shadows, the world from which they are absent loses all consistency and concreteness, that is, every sympathetic connection, and becomes a world of shadow and fear, a world without relations, an abstract world. Abstract art is the art of the abstract individual, the art of the mass. For modern painting, whether we are thrown into an abstract objectivism or an abstract intellectualism, everything, as with King Midas, becomes gold.

The terror of freedom estranges us from the world and peoples it with monsters. If the individual creator has no fixed limits, the "ombre peureuse" seek instead within limits the only possible defense from unleashed solitude; and adore every limit, the only certainty for he who lacks any support. And the painting that is born from this world is an attempt at salvation, whether it is resigned or rebellious, if it shows us

Les geographies solennelles des limites humaines.[4]

Such is Picasso, a gigantic (literally: from the time, not of men, but of Giants) attempt, gigantically impossible, to exit from the inhuman limits of abstraction, to break the enchantment with violence, to

---

2. "The prominent light / In the sky no longer the mirror of the sun" (ibid.).
3. "And the shadows defend me from my timid shadow" (ibid.).
4. "The solemn geography of human limits" (Paul Éluard, "À Pablo Picasso," in *Oeuvres complètes*, 1:499.

rediscover human limits. It is an attempt that has always failed and always been repeated, describing in infinite ways the infinite aspects of a world become monstrous, circumnavigating the crystalline island of petrified things, beating in vain against all doors of the forbidden universe, in case one of them answers with a terrestrial sound, ferociously illuminating all the dark corners, searching in all places and all times—and above all full of humanity in this desperate attempt, predestined to ruin. Heroic warrior of a world that is only heroic, but a poet for the persistent desperation to escape from the self. But in this continuous attempt to attain an impossible reality, with only the magic of the will, every figure in its most infinite diversity is identical with all the others, because the will has only one meaning: a simple meaning. Every painting is a cry, an onslaught against invisible enchanted walls: and the cry is a point without dimensions. All is one, because two are not given where a relationship is not possible. Where the Hero is not Eros. The infinite aspects of the world crystallize in the monstrous idols, substantially identical with the infinite, inexistent Gods.

This continuous creation of idols is also an attempt at magical liberation; the image should free us from God, or at least from solitude; inhabiting the void of the world, giving form to ambiguous things, freeing us from the terror of the shapeless and the uncertain. We carry complexes in our consciousness if we are afraid of the dark: but if we are not free, no light of conscience will free us: even rationalistic surrealism is an attempt destined to fail.

Estranged from the world, we seek refuge in dreams as the only real thing; but the dreams reflect back to us an image equally estranged, as we are to ourselves.

The fear of man, that is, the fear of painting, is the meaning of contemporary painting. To flee from our own human nature, what a display of ingenuity and heroism; to flee from painting, what marvelous efforts! Perhaps never before have we seen works so ingenious, techniques so refined, searches so profound, attempts so titanic.

Not so are its imitations in places where, although the crisis existed, it was not profoundly and sincerely felt, but accepted as a style or a formal imperative; there where those which, in painters of different training and tradition were the multiple and equivalent

expressions of an anguished impossibility, were considered pictorial points of arrival; or there where we were hiding so as not to see
the old styles of painting were being repeated for fear of the new
and the void or nothingness. Here there was fear of painting in the
more trivial sense: that is, a lack of courage and a faithfulness to an
eternal academy.

> . . . et des mains trop fidèles
> pour dépeupler un monde dont je suis absent.[5]

This empty world, which was feared to be left empty, was therefore not inhabited by heroic monsters, but with traditional figures
and forms, hiding the fear with classicism and irony, and embracing, of that tragedy, only the schemes, like Arcadian disguises. But
the crisis is not concealed with eclecticism nor by looking back.

Picasso and the others have created the images of contemporary
desolation, the images of Fear: and without fear of their appearance,
they have given us the changing forms of the transient Gods of our
age. A barbarous and religious art is thus born, with no possibility
of development unless monotonous: other births have not arrived.
The future is prepared not with paintbrushes, but within the heart
of men; and men, who have followed their Gods to the pit of hell,
yearn to return to the light and to sprout like a subterranean seed.
From the summit of fear is born a hope, a ray of light of consensus
of man and things. With the death of the Gods, the human person
is recreated. Can death and night subvert fate? If art truly indicates
the future, and if we can read it on the face and the gestures of man,
the war of man with himself is finished. And perhaps is born he who
prepares, in his paintings, the annunciation of the end of the separation and the loving resurrection of a painting without terror.

—Carlo Levi
1 July 1942

---

5. "And hands too loyal / To depopulate a world from which I am absent" (Éluard,
   "Giorgio De Chirico," 1:144).

Select Bibliography

Selected Works in Italian by Carlo Levi

Cristo si è fermato a Eboli. Turin: Einaudi, 1945.
Paura della libertà. Turin: Einaudi, 1946.
L'orologio. Turin: Einaudi, 1950.
Le parole sonno pietre. Turin: Einaudi, 1955
Il futuro ha un cuore antico. Turin: Einaudi, 1956.
La doppia notte dei tigli. Turin: Einaudi, 1959.
Un volto che ci somiglia. Turin: Einaudi, 1960
Tutto il miele è finito. Turin: Einaudi, 1964.
Coraggio dei mitti: Scritti contemporanei, 1922–1974. Ed. Gigliola De Donato. Bari: De Donato Editore, 1975.
Contadini e Luigini: Testi e disegni di Carlo Levi. Ed. Leonardo Sacco. Rome, Matera: Basilicata Editore, 1975.
Amicizia. Storia di un vecchio poeta e di un giovane canarino (quasi un racconto) 1951. With Umberto Saba. Milan: Mondori, 1976.
Quaderno a cancelli. Turin: Einaudi, 1979.
L'altro mondo è il Mezzogiorno. Ed. Leonardo Sacco. Reggio Calabria: Casa del Libro, 1980.
Poesie inedite, 1934–1946. Rome: Mancosu, 1990.
E questo il "carcer tetro"? Lettere dal carcere, 1934–1935. Ed. Daniela Ferraro. Genoa: Il Melangolo, 1991.
Carissimo Puck: Lettere d'amore e di vita, 1945–1969. Ed. Sergio D'Amaro. Rome: Mancosu, 1994.
Pensiero politico. Ritratti, monotipi e disegni dal carcere. Ferrara: Corbo Editore, 1995.
Il bambino del 7 luglio. Dal neofascismo ai fatti di Reggio Emilia. Ed. Sandro Gerbi. Cava dei Tirreni: Avagliano, 1996.
L'invenzione della verità. Ed. Valeria Berani and Maria Grignani. Alessandria: Edizioni dell'Orso, 1998.

Le mille patrie. Uomini, fatti, paesi d'Italia. Ed. Gigliola De Donato. Rome: Donzelli, 2000.

Paesaggi 1926–1974. Lirismo e metamorfosi della natura. Ed. Pia Vivarelli. Corigliano Calabro Scalo: Meridiana, 2001.

Prima e dopo le parole. Scritti e discorsi sulla letteratura. Ed. Gigliola De Donato and Rosalba Galvagno. Rome: Donzelli, 2001.

Scritti politici. Ed. David Bidussa. Turin: Einaudi, 2001.

Lo specchio. Scritti di critica d'arte. Ed. Pia Vivarelli. Rome: Donzelli, 2001.

Le traccie della memoria. Ed. Maria Pagliara. Rome: Donzelli, 2002.

Roma fuggitiva: una città e i suoi dintorni. Ed. Gigliola De Donato. Rome: Donzelli, 2002.

Un dolente amore per la vita: Conversazioni radiofoniche e interviste. Ed. Luigi M. Lombardi Satriani and Letizia Bindi. Rome: Donzelli, 2003.

Discorsi parlamentare. Bologna: Il Mulino, 2003.

Il pianeta senza confini. Prose di viaggio. Ed. Vanna Zaccaro. Rome: Donzelli, 2003.

Verso i sud del mondo. Carlo Levi a cento anni della nascita. Ed. Gigliola De Donato. Rome: Donzelli, 2003.

Contro la guerra. Carlo Levi al popolo di Bari. Ed. Domenico Rodolfo. Fasano: Schena, 2003.

La ragione dei topi. Storie di animali. Ed. Gigliola De Donato. Rome: Donzelli, 2004.

Il dovere dei tempi. Prose politiche e civili. Ed. Luisa Montevecchi. Rome: Donzelli, 2005.

La strana idea da battersi per la libertà. Dai giornali della liberazione (1944–1946). Ed. Filippo Benfante. Santa Maria C.V. (CE): Spartaco, 2005.

Il seme nascosto. Tocca ai contadini, ai piccoli, agli ultimi a uccidere il serpente. Ed. Aldo Cormio. Bari: Palomar di Alternative, 2006.

Works in English by Carlo Levi

Christ Stopped at Eboli. Trans. Frances Frenaye. New York: Farrar, Straus & Company: 1947, 1963, 1974; with a new introduction by Mark Rotella, 2006.

Of Fear and Freedom. Trans. Adolphe Gourevitch. New York: Farrar, Straus & Company, 1950.

The Watch. Trans. Frances Frenaye. New York: Farrar, Straus & Young, 1951; South Royalton, Vt.: Steerforth Italia, 1999.

Words Are Stones. Trans. Angus Davidson. New York: Farrar, Straus & Company, 1958.

Eternal Italy. With János Reismann. Rome: Viking Press, 1959.

The Linden Trees. Trans. Joseph M. Bernstein. New York: Knopf, 1962.

Fleeting Rome: In Search of La Dolce Vita. Trans. Antony Shugaar. Chichester, West Sussex: John Wiley & Sons, 2004.

Words Are Stones. Trans. Antony Shugaar. London: Hesperus, 2005.

Selected Secondary Works

Acetoso, Raffaella, Francesco Allegrucci, and Luigi Amedeo de Biase, eds. *Dalla biblioteca di Levi e Saba*, Perugia: Quattroemme, 2005.

Arouimi, Michel. *Magies de Levi. L'expérience picturale et littéraire de Carlo Levi*. Fasano: Schena, 2006.

———. "Nerval, Carlo Levi, Rimbaud." *Revue des sciences humaines* no. 278 (2005): 101–21.

Baldassaro, Lawrence. "*Paura della libertà*: Carlo Levi's Unfinished Preface." *Italica* 72, no. 2 (1995): 143–54.

Bini, Daniela. "Women of the South and the Art of Carlo Levi." *Forum Italicum* 37, no. 1 (2003): 103–21.

Bronzini, Giovanni Battista. *Il viaggio antropologico di Carlo Levi*. Bari: Dedalo, 1996.

Camon, Ferdinando. "Sulle orme di Carlo Levi." *Belfagor* 59, no. 5 (2004): 597–603.

Carducci, Nicola. *Storia intellettuale di Carlo Levi*. Lecce: Pensa Multimedia, 1999.

Carlo Levi. Riletture. A special Iissue of *Meridiana: Rivista di storia e scienze sociali*. Vol. 53 (September 2006).

Caserta, Giovanni. *Nuova introduzione a Carlo Levi*. Venosa, Potenza: Osanna, 1996.

Catani, R. D. "Structure and Style as Expression: The Works of Carlo Levi and Their Poetic Ideology." *Italica* 46, no. 2 (Summer 1979): 213–29.

Collura, Laura. "Fleeting Rome—in Search of 'La Dolce Vita' by Carlo Levi." *Times Literary Supplement* no. 5303 (2004).

D'Amaro, Sergio. *Il mondo di Carlo Levi*. Rome: Mancosu, 1998.

De Donato, Gigliola, ed. *Carlo Levi. Il tempo e la durata in "Cristo si è fermato a Eboli."* Rome: Farenheit 451, 2000.

———, ed. *Carlo Levi nella storia e nella cultura italiana*. Manduria: Piero Lacaita, 1993.

———. *Le parole del reale. Ricerche sulla prosa di Carlo Levi*. Bari: Dedalo, 1998.

———. *Saggio sul Carlo Levi*. Bari: De Donato, 1974.

De Donato, Gigliola, and Sergio D'Amaro. *Un torinese del sud: Carlo Levi. Una biografia*. Milan: Baldini & Castoldi, 2005.

Falaschi, Giovanni. *Carlo Levi*. Florence: La Nuova Italia, 1978.

Faleschini-Lerner, Giovanna. "Carlo Levi's *L'orologio*: A Revolution in Words and Images." In *Creative Interventions: The Role of the Intellectual in Contemporary Italian Culture*, ed. Eugenio Bolongaro, Rita Gagliano, and Mark Epstein. Cambridge: Cambridge Scholars Press, forthcoming.

———. "Francesco Rosi's 'Cristo si è fermato a Eboli': Toward a Cinema of Painting." *Italica* (forthcoming).

———. "'Ogni segno è pittura': Carlo Levi's Visual Poetics." Ph.D. diss., University of Pennsylvania, 2006.

Finocchiaro, Giampiero. "Carlo Levi: Paesaggio a Iercara." *Nuova Antologia* 138, no. 2225 (2003): 335–45.

———. *Tornare a Isnello. Carlo Levi e il grande viaggio del sindaco di New York.* Casalecchio di Reno: Arianna, 2006.

Friguglietti, Mark. "Carlo Levi: The Structure and Significance of *Cristo si è fermato a Eboli.*" Ph.D. diss., Indiana University, 1997.

Galvagno, Rosalba. *Carlo Levi, Narciso e la costruzione della realtà.* Florence: Olschki, 2004.

Ghiazza, Silvana. *Carlo Levi e Umberto Saba. Storia di un'amicizia.* Bari: Dedalo, 2003.

———. "Carlo Levi e Umberto Saba." *Italianistica* 32, no. 3, (2003): 497–99.

Guerard, Albert. "Carlo Levi's Theology." *The Nation* 170, no. 7 (February 18, 1950): 158.

Miccinese, Mario. *Invito alla lettura di Carlo Levi.* Milan: Mursia. 1998.

Misan, Jacques. "Testimonial: Trois Recontres avec Carlo Levi." *Italica* 52, no. 1 (Spring 1975): 90–94.

Napolillo, Vincenzo. *Carlo Levi. Dall'antifascismo al mito contadino.* Cosenza: Brenner, 1984.

"Nell'universo di Carlo Levi: Convegno di studio per il centenario della nascita." *Forum Italicum* 37, no. 1 (2003): 236–52.

Pellegrini, Glauco. *Nel sole di Villa Strohl-Fern.* Venice: Corbo e Fiore, 1985.

Raffa, Guy. "Carlo Levi's Sacred Art of Healing," *Annali d'Italianistica* 15 (1997): 203–20.

Ragghianti, Carlo Ludovico. *Carlo Levi.* Florence: Edizioni U, 1948.

Rosi, Francesco. *Cristo si è fermato a Eboli. Dal libro di Carlo Levi al film.* Turin: Testo & Immagine, 1996.

Russo, Giovanni. "Carlo Levi e Umberto Saba." *Nuova Antologia* 138, no. 2226 (2003): 151–54.

———. *Lettera a Carlo Levi.* Rome: Editori Riuniti, 2001.

———. *Il paese di Carlo Levi.* Bari: Laterza, 1985.

Sacco, Leonardo. *L'orologio della Repubblica: Carlo Levi e il caso Italia.* Matera: Basilicata, 1999.

Siani, Cosma. "Carlo Levi interprete di Laurence Sterne." *L'indice dei libri del mese* 20, no. 9 (2003): 10.

Sirovich, Ghislana. *L'azione politica di Carlo Levi.* Rome: Il Ventaglio, 1988.

Speduto, Donato. "La futilità del tutto: Emanuele Severino e Carlo Levi." *Sapienza* 57, no. 4 (2004): 485–89.

Squarotti, Giorgio B. *L'orologio d'Italia. Carlo Levi e altri racconti.* Ragusa: Libroitaliano, 2001.

Testaguzza, Adrio. *Carlo Levi scrittore.* Florence: CDA libri, 1969.

Vitelli, Franco, ed. *Il germoglio sotto la scorza: Carlo Levi vent'anni dopo.* Cava de' Tirreni (Salerno): Avagliano, 1998.

-Ward, David. *Antifascisms: Cultural Politics in Italy, 1943–1946: Benedetto Croce and the Liberals, Carlo Levi and the "Actionists."* Madison, N.J.: Fairleigh Dickinson University Press, 1996.

———. *Gli italiani e la paura della libertà.* Florence: La Nuova Italia, 2004.

Zaccaro, Vanna. *Un viaggiatore allo specchio. Tre studi su Carlo Levi.* Lecce: Pensa Multimedia, 2002.

Painting Catalogues

Carlo Levi: Mostra Antologica. Mantua, Palazzo de Te, September–October 1974. Milan: Electa Editrice, 1974.

Carlo Levi, 1928–1937. Ed. Mario Micheli. Milan: Galleria trentadue, 1977.

Carlo Levi si ferma a Firenze. Ed. Carlo Ludovico Ragghianti. Florence: Fratelli Alinari, 1977.

Carlo Levi. Disegni, 1920–1935. Venice: Corbo e Fiore, 1980.

Carlo Levi. Disegni dal carcere, 1934. Rome: De Luca, 1983.

Carlo Levi e la Lucania. Dipinti del confino, 1935–1936. Matera, Centro Carlo Levi, Palazzo Lanfranchi, 16 June–21 October 1990. Ed. Stefano De Duca. Rome: De Duca Edizione d'Arte, 1990.

Carlo Levi: Il futuro ha un cuore antico. Opere scelte dal 1922 al 1972. Museo di Palazzo Venezia-Roma. Ed. Francesco Ruggiero and Paola Sacerdoti. Rome: CGIL, 1993.

Galleria dei ritratti. Corigliano Calabro Scalo: Meridiana, 2000.

Cultura artistica in Basilicata. La pittura di Carlo Levi. Naples: Paparo Edizioni, 2002.

Carlo Levi inedito. Milazzo: SPES, 2003.

Carlo Levi. Ausgewählte Werke 1926–1974. Ed. Pia Vivarelli and Micheli Saponaro. Matera: Soprintendenza P.S.A.D. della Basilicata, 2003.

Carlo Levi. Gli anni fiorentini, 1941–1945, Comitato Nazionale per le Celebrazioni del Centenario della Nascita di Carlo Levi. Rome: Donzelli, 2003.

Carlo Levi a Matera. 199 dipinti e una scultura. Corigliano Calabro Scalo: Meridiana, 2005.

Carlo Levi. "Siamo liberati." Cinquanta opere dalla Resistenza alla Repubblica. Catalogue of exhibition in Naples, 29 September–29 October 2005. Corigliano Calabro Scalo: Meridiana, 2005.